For my husband, Don,
who has faithfully and patiently seen me through this journey
and all the other metamorphoses of the last twenty-five years.

RCIA
SPIRITUALITY

Formation for the Catechumenate Team

Barbara Hixon
with reflection questions by Gael Gensler

Resource Publications, Inc.
San Jose, California

Adventure into Mayhem and
ublications, Inc.

Reprint Department
Resource Publications, Inc.
160 E. Virginia Street #290
San Jose, CA 95112-5876
1-408-286-8506 (voice)
1-408-287-8748 (fax)

Library of Congress Cataloging in Publication Data
Hixon, Barbara, 1934-
    RCIA spirituality : formation for the catechumenate team /
Barbara Hixon with reflection questions by Gael Gensler. — Rev. ed.
        p.   cm.
    Rev. ed. of: RCIA ministry. c1989.
    Includes bibliographical references.
    ISBN 0-89390-399-X
    1. Initiation rites—Religious aspects—Catholic Church.
2. Catholic Church—United States—Membership.
3. Catechumens—Religious life. I. Gensler, Gael. II. Hixon, Barbara,
1934 RCIA ministry. III. Title.
BX2045.IffH59   1997
264'.020813—dc21   96-29997

Printed in the United States of America

2 3 4 5 6 | 06 05 04 03 02

Editorial directors: Kenneth Guentert, Nick Wagner
Prepress manager: Elizabeth J. Asborno
Editorial assistant: Michelle Moreland
Production assistant: David Dunlap

Contents

Part One: The Precatechumenal Mentality

FOCAL ISSUES: inquiry and evangelism

Part Two: The Catechumenal Mentality

FOCAL ISSUES: journey and conversion

Part Three: Purification and Enlightenment

FOCAL ISSUES: sin and salvation

Part Four: Sacraments of Initiation – The Baptismal Mentality

FOCAL ISSUES: death and resurrection

Part Five: The Mystagogical Mentality

FOCAL ISSUES: sacrament and mission

Preface to the Revised Edition

Welcome! You and your companions are about to begin an unimaginable journey. This journey is a dialogue revolving around the implementation of the *Rite of Christian Initiation of Adults*. This dialogue requires time, energy, and commitment, but then, you have already agreed to that or you would not be reading this. The main tools for this dialogue include two publications: this book, *RCIA Spirituality: Formation for the Catechumenate Team*, and the text of the rite itself, *The Rite of Christian Initiation of Adults*. The dialogue also includes your experience of implementing the rite and what is presently your parish process. As you enter this dialogue, you will find questions and comments that bear reflection and discussion among the team. The dialogue will affirm some of what you are already doing in your parish catechumenal process; it will challenge some of what you are doing; and it will provide insight into the process and its principles. The dialogue begins with two questions:

- What are your hopes for this dialogue?

- What questions do you bring to the discussion?

Gael Gensler

Acknowledgments

When Jim Dunning received the finished copy of my manuscript, he telephoned me. "I see the baby is born," he quipped. He was right—writing a book was much like bearing a child. In my case it was more like the old-style home births, not with a large professional team and clinic at your service but with a few trusted and experienced friends who stand vigil with you and wait quietly to assist and to comfort. To these I give heartfelt thanks.

The creative process first required a focusing of vision and the courage to trust that vision. The milieu that supported those processes for me was my two years of study at Corpus Christi Center for Liturgical Studies in Phoenix. It was a time of new vision and a discovery that I could trust my old vision. It was also a time of affirmation and maturation. In the end, it was Fr. John Gallen, SJ, the dean and mentor of the Center, who encouraged me to pursue the possibility of publication. John did for me what no one else in the church has done for me in my lifetime of Catholic service: he heard me, he honored my gifts, and he encouraged their use in a concrete and do-able way. He empowered me. Thanks, John!

One cannot have a baby at home without a midwife. Mine was Jean Wever. She stood by me through it all: held my hand, helped me to breathe, and told me when to push harder. More than that, Jean is a soul-friend whose honesty and insight kept me on track. Her encouragement convinced me that the baby would be beautiful. Thanks, friend! Thanks also to Char Walker, who willingly offered moral support and technical assistance with red pen and computer savvy.

Finally, special thanks to Fr. Jim Lopresti, who was the first of the Forum team to encourage me to write; thanks to Fr. Jim Dunning; thanks to both for happily assuring me that, in fact, the baby is beautiful.

Barbara Hixon

Thanks to the following for permission to reprint copyrighted material:

The Scripture quotations contained herein are from the New Revised Standard Version of the Bible, copyrighted, 1989 by the Division of Christian Education of the National Council of the Churches of Christ in the United States of America, and are used by permission. All rights reserved.

Excerpts from the English translation of *Lectionary for Mass* © 1969, 1981, International Committee on English in the Liturgy, Inc. (ICEL); excerpts from the English translation of *Documents on the Liturgy, 1963-1979: Conciliar, Papal, and Curial Texts* © 1982, ICEL; excerpts from the English translation of *Rite of Christian Initiation of Adults* © 1985, ICEL. All rights reserved.

Excerpts from *Music in Catholic Worship* © 1978 United States Catholic Conference (USCC), Washington DC 20017 are used with permission.

From *Made, Not Born: New Perspectives on Christian Initiation and the Catechumenate* by the Murphey Center, Center for Pastoral Liturgy. © 1959 by the University of Notre Dame Press. Used by permission.

From *The God Who Fell From Heaven* by John Shea. © Copyright 1979 Tabor Publishing, a division of RCL Enterprises, Inc.

From *Christian Initiation Resource Reader* vol. 4. © 1984 Wm. H. Sadlier Press. Used with permission.

Reprinted from "Paraphrase of the Exsultet," by Gabe Huck. *The Three Days,* © 1981. Archdiocese of Chicago: Liturgy Training Publications. 1800 N. Hermitage Ave., Chicago, IL 60622-1101. 1-800-933-1800. All rights reserved. Used with permission.

Introduction

James Fowler describes faith as a way of "leaning into life" (92). The first time I heard that, a picture popped into my mind of Alice (of Wonderland fame) leaning through the looking glass. Had it not been for her eagerness to see where barely viewed passages might lead and what lay hidden behind things in the Looking-glass House, she might never have discovered the mystery and life beyond that glittering reflection of her ordinary world. From the sitting room, the Looking-glass House seemed to repeat all that she presumed about life. But when she leaned into the looking glass, Alice found herself face to face with an entirely new dimension of reality. As it turned out, all her values were reversed, and she discovered a whole new way of being that frequently caught her by surprise and of which she was never quite in control. Faith and conversion are like that—leading us into a world of topsy-turvy values and the possibility of the Other.

Anyone involved in the Rite of Christian Initiation of Adults should beware. There ought to be a caution label on the cover of these rites: "Warning! This is a journey into mayhem and mystery. It may be dangerous to your status quo!" Those determined to proceed should have a bit of Alice in them. For without that willingness to lean through material order into

1

the messiness of mystery, it is difficult to discover for oneself or to lay open to others anything except the image of one's own world mirrored back. I write this book for those catechumenate team members and ministers and for all who are struggling to be Alices but haven't quite leaned through the looking glass.

There has been a fair amount written about the *Rite of Christian Initiation of Adults* since the document's promulgation in English in 1974, and the North American Forum for the Catechumenate has been a powerful catalyst in its implementation. Still, it seems to be a struggle for the American church at large to really get the hang of it. My experience doesn't extend to the universal church, but my guess is that we Americans are not alone in our struggle. There is good reason for that. The Rite of Christian Initiation of Adults is not just a lovely new way to process converts. The document calls for a new way of being church, demanding a complete re-evaluation of how one is Christian. Ralph Keifer's often-quoted insight into the radical nature of the rite is worth pondering once again:

> Historically and culturally speaking, [the rites are] a massive rejection of the presuppositions both of pastoral practice and of most churchgoers regarding the true meaning of church membership. This is a revolution quite without precedent, because the Catholic church has never at any time in its history done such violence to its ritual practice as to make its rites so wholly incongruous with its concrete reality. Such an act is either a statement that rite is wholly irrelevant, or a statement that the church is willing to change, and to change radically that concrete reality. Such an approach is either suicide or prophecy of a very high order.

Given the promise of the continued presence of Christ and his Spirit with the church for "all days," I presume she is not suicidal. I do believe that what we are talking about is prophecy of a very high order indeed.

The collegial voice of the church in this document is like that of the prophet, John the Baptist, crying in the desert: "Change your hearts! The kingdom of God is at hand." Will we hear that voice? Or will we silence it by presenting it on a platter from the head up, cut off from the body? We as individuals and as parishes are in danger of doing just that: of detaching the head from the body of initiation, perhaps because the whole of the message is far too powerful and personally ours for comfort. If we wish to disengage ourselves, personally and as whole communities, from the game of prophet-killing, we need to accept without grudge the message that it is we who must change and that as a people our marriage to modern culture is an adulterous one. We need to repent of uncritical appropriation within the church of these less-than-Christian values. Instead, we must have in us the mind of Christ Jesus. This means that as church we must cease grasping at being God and be willing to be known as human, to be emptied of pomposity, and to serve in humble obedience. It means that death, not self-preservation, is the bottom line. For centuries, our working assumption in Christian initiation has been that converting is about conforming to the church. But these prophetic rites are calling us back to the truth that Christian initiation is about conforming to Christ and that this is not all done, but just begun, in the baptismal waters. The rite also calls us to ritual honesty, to *be* what we celebrate, to drop the ecclesial *persona* which in the past has suggested a transformation more grand than the reality it masked. This reality, as Keifer points out, has been a symbiotic pact between the established church and modern cultural values characterized by ritual which "made few demands on the individual and virtually none on the congregation...[a fact] made brutally clear by the baptismal scene in *The Godfather*."

The *Rite of Christian Initiation of Adults* is the most radical document to hit Catholics in centuries. We are doomed to failure if we approach this rite with our toes dug in to what we regard as familiar Catholic turf. The rite is frankly not concerned with the proselytizing of Catholicism but with the making of Christians. This call to conversion begins with the faithful. In paragraph four of the introduction to this rite, the unsettling question is asked of the initiating community: Who are we and whom do we presume ourselves to be in light of the paschal mystery? Our failure will be assured if we continue to ignore this paragraph, which grounds the whole process in the renewed conversion of the faithful. Discomforting as this may be, the rite rests on the assumption that those who minister in the initiation of Christians must be no less than Christian themselves. Christian communities and catechumenate teams must be prepared to be uprooted, to let go of familiar ground. Letting go of comfortable connections is life-threatening. This is the real issue in implementing the rites. People aren't crazy about laying the life they cling to on the line. But that's what it takes. Our propensity is to hang on to familiar ground, to simply create another domesticated and non-prophet program dressed up as initiation. This happens because pastors and parishes and team members have not understood that initiation rites demand the conversion of the whole church, not just those who newly approach her.

Therefore, I believe it is crucial that we initiation ministers debunk the presumption that we are the "do-ers" and begin to suspect that we too are the "do-ees." We frequently use the language of being fellow travelers; we say that we are journeying with the catechumens. We need to confront ourselves: How often is this only lip service? As initiation ministers, are we really journeying, really moved from the fixed attitudes we began with? Or are our old presumptions in fact our continuing *modus operandi*? In our past experience, the church's operative mode in the initiation and formation of its members has been the transmission of ideas, not life transformation. But the Rite of Christian Initiation of Adults demands much more than that. It says plainly that we are in fact a pilgrim church, that no one has arrived, and that we must indeed journey together. Being in initiation ministry is something like being an airplane pilot. We can't get the folks to their destination without making the same trip ourselves, sharing the smooth and the bumpy times, entering into the same space and experience, taking the same risks. Initiation ministers, clerical or lay, are not in the tower directing takeoff and landing. *God is.* Our desire to give directions instead of taking the trip is what domesticates initiation into just another well-crafted human program which has precious little to do with conversion—ours or anybody else's.

The difference between the Rite of Christian Initiation and convert classes is not simply format or "process." The major difference is that a rite calls one into a subject-to-subject encounter, demanding a vulnerability that puts at risk the understanding of one's own identity. A ritual is by nature communal; the rite of initiation calls both comer and receiver into mutual conversion. The problem is that these words can be said over and over again, and we can all assent to these words intellectually. But words without experience do not transform. In order for a book to effect a real understanding of what initiation is all about, it must create an experience.

How, I asked myself, can one write words that are also an experience? Poetry, of course, is the only real answer to that question. I did, according to my ability, the next best thing. Through metaphor and Gospel images, I have attempted to at least crack open a small, slitted vision of the enormous and mysterious adventure we are called to through conversion into Christ. Hopefully, a certain mentality has been exposed out of which the Rite of Christian Initiation of Adults can be truly Christ-initiating. A mentality cannot be transmitted like a germ. Rather, what is needed is a "discovery attitude," an internal process which begins with an openness to the possibility that we don't have it all, a willingness to search. Having found something new, a discoverer must discern what is of value and take steps to appropriate it. It is my hope that this book will give encouragement and aid to initiation ministers and to all others who are open to discovery.

"Mentality" is a milieu that colors our whole view of things and determines which way we have the courage to lean. Initiation is an invitation to lean through the reflection of our cultural values into the realm of Christian folly. St. Paul, after his own journey into mystery, marvels that we see now as in a mirror, but *then* face to face (1 Cor 13:12). I would like to suggest that initiation can be a journey into "then," a journey *through* the mirror, a journey into a world of other values, reversed priorities, a place of complete turnaround. With Alice and with Paul, these radical, prophetic rites can draw us past the reflection of our own image into the place where we can meet the Other face to face. The "then" Paul talks about is not a matter of time but of vision.

For Discussion

- How do you describe faith?

- How do you understand James Fowler's definition of faith as "leaning into life"?

- In what ways have you experienced this description of faith? When did it happen? Who was involved?

- Read the general introduction to the ritual text. Pay particular attention to last section of paragraph 2, which begins "thus the three sacraments of initiation closely combine...." How do you understand this paragraph?

- What is the "mission" of Jesus Christ?

- What is the place of the Catholic church in relation to this "mission" of Jesus Christ?

- What values do you see reflected in the statement on page 3 that "as church we must cease grasping at being God and be willing to be known as human"? What is involved for you? for your team? for your parish?

- Read paragraph 4 of the rite. How do you understand the role of team and the role of the parish in the making of Christians?

- What is it you need to "let go" of in order to work with this process?

- Who is the team? How do you relate to one other? How does the team understand its role in the conversion of process?

- Discuss the goal of the process. Is it to add members to your parish or about becoming a disciple of Jesus Christ? Does the team place more emphasis on information or on transformation?

- On a scale of 1 (membership, information) to 10 (discipleship, transformation), where do you place your parish process? Why? What propels the members of the team to continue to minister in the process?

- In your parish, who does the initiating? Why? Who does not do the initiating? Why?

- How can you as a team keep from getting in the way of the Spirit? How do you bolster the work of the Spirit?

Part One

The Precatechumenal Mentality

"Pressing your nose against the glass"

FOCAL ISSUES: inquiry and evangelism

What Is the Precatechumenal Mentality?

> When Jesus turned and saw them following, he said to
> them, "What are you looking for?" They said to him,
> "Rabbi (which translated means Teacher), where are you
> staying?" He said to them, "Come and see." They came
> and saw where he was staying, and they remained with him
> that day (Jn 1:38-39).

Here unfolds the first precatechumenate, graphically drawn in these four short sentences. It isn't what you would call a neat program. There's a question, another question for an answer, and an answer that doesn't answer but invites. It seems that pressing into mystery gives questioning the primacy, leaving answers open-ended. "Response-able" wondering is the key: "What are you looking for?"

The *Rite of Christian Initiation of Adults* calls this questioning process *inquiry; evangelization* is the answer that invites. This is the language the catechumenate team must deal with and interpret. What connotations do these words raise? At first glance, inquiry appears to be a comfort zone. As Americans we are at home with problem solving, with answering questions (including ones that were never asked). The easy assumption is that inquiry is primarily a time to dispense information, answers to the asked and unasked questions. And the next trap is to assume that we know which information is wanted or needed. Such assumptions once again give common wisdom occasion to prove itself: that to assume makes "fools" of you and me! For in the context of initiation, inquiry proves to be paradoxical. The "inquirer" might ask fewer questions than the team, and the primary goal of this period is not so much to find right answers but to *raise the right questions.* Opened-ended questions, not categorical answers, are of the essence. The heart of this inquiry is discovering the way we, as disciples, ought to "be" in the world. But not unlike Hamlet, we fear to press the issue of being, the mysterious possibility of the dream, that which resides beyond our present way of life. Indeed, there's the rub! In the context of initiation, inquiry takes on that mysterious, deeper, and perhaps more scary dimension. And it is always double-edged. Neither inquirer nor respondent is safe from the question; it challenges both to peer beyond the surface, where there are no pat answers.

Then there is evangelization. American Catholics generally are uncomfortable and self-conscious with the concept of evangelization. We have visions of fanatics on street corners grumbling at the passers-by and waving signs of "Jesus Saves." We have been quite satisfied, thank you, with the more quiet and less distressing process of birthing and baptizing our babies. The thought of having to share with other *adults* the Evangel, the "Good News" of Christ incarnated in our lives, is very scary stuff for most Catholics. Consequently, the greatest temptation of catechumenate teams is to ignore evangelism by taking refuge first in the paper forest of information forms, initial interviews, and baptismal records, and then in a program of instruction camouflaged by periods of socializing and group discussions. In other words, evangelizing, exploring the possibility that the dream might be good news, discovering the Christ dimension in our personal story is simply skipped over. Instructing, we understand; storytelling is suspiciously impractical (what does it *do*, anyway?) Nonetheless, the church persists: during this time of evangelization our story, the Good News, must be told. Otherwise, the catechesis of the following period will be without foundation. For those who are left-brained and wringing their hands, here's the logic: the Greek root of catechesis means "to echo," it presupposes a Word first spoken aloud, a voicing to be heard again and again. Without evangelization, the first hearing of The Story, catechumenal catechesis is an empty echo.

All well and good. But that still leaves those of us in the ditches squirming in discomfort: how do we go about this evangelizing? Who really are the inquirers: us or them? Are there only questions? What about answers? What is the precatechumenal *mentality*?

For Discussion

- Describe what happens in your parish regarding the precatechumenate period. To help you do this, answer these questions: Who facilitates the sessions? Where and when do the sessions take place? How often do they meet? How is the parish invited to participate? How are new inquirers integrated into sessions, or are they told to wait until the next group begins? Who determines the agenda of each session?

- RCIA paragraph 8 states that the whole process is to bear a "markedly paschal nature." What does that mean for the precatechumenate period?

- How does the team understand the term "evangelization"?

- The precatechumenate is focused on "first faith" (RCIA 42) and "initial conversion" (RCIA 37). How does what you as a parish do in this process support this?

The Jesus Approach

Fortunately, Jesus offers a straightforward model, graciously recounted for us in John's Gospel. The scenario is a human one: a couple of the Baptist's disciples, made curious by John's remark about this passerby, fell in behind him to see where he was going. What follows is the "Jesus approach" to inquiry and evangelization.

The basic elements of the story are these. Jesus noticed that someone was following him. Turning around, he asked the natural question: "What do you want; what are you looking for?" They counter with another question, run-of-the-mill and non-risky: "Where are you staying?" (They don't let on that they *really* want to know his lifestyle, what kind of person he is, what makes him different). Jesus understood the questions that weren't asked, but without comment or dissertation, simply invited them: "Come and see." They came and saw, and they remained with him.

Jesus Saw Them

Noticing tentative footsteps that approach from behind is a special kind of hospitality. It requires an awareness of presence and an openness to the unasked question; it precludes the paranoia of fearful self-protectionism. Being approached from behind also demands a willingness to turn around, and to be an inquirer (what are you looking for?) before being a teacher. It is an attitude of humility in its true sense: being *humus*, earth enriched by deaths of its own, loose and open to receive new life. This is not simply poetic commentary upon a Gospel phrase, but a challenge to our basic approach. Jesus' behavior stands in radical contrast to all the "isms" our culture makes us heir to: individualism, privatism, clericalism, proselytism etc. Deep reflection upon Christ's graceful hospitality will go a long way toward clarifying and effecting the precatechumenal mission.

Recognizing these behavioral patterns as elements of hospitality is not easy for the western mind, which is action oriented. We think of ourselves as the doers and the "welcomee" as the receiver. Jesus modeled the more subtle, eastern mentality: that of receptivity. It is he who is the receiver. He reaches out; the one who approaches is gift.

Our strongly action-oriented hospitality sometimes offers everything to the inquirer except reverence to that person. Under the premise that we are the givers and they are the takers, the unspoken assumption is that all who have come are somehow deficient and await the cure, the Catholic prescription. The corollary to that is that the faster we apply the remedy, the sooner they'll be well. Such Catholic elitism has no basis in the Gospel. By contrast, Jesus' noticing is a gracious respect for each person whoever they are, however they come, and whatever they bring. It is an attitude of sensitivity to the individual approach. More than that, Jesus is keenly aware of his own need: that without these (and others like them) the "why" of his life is aborted. His mission approaches from behind; it is time for him to turn around.

The same need and the same mission is ours. We must turn around and take notice. They approach from behind.

What Are You Looking For? Where Are You Staying?

Having noticed them, the natural question is "Why are you here? What are you looking for?" The initial communication Jesus models here is certainly off the cuff, but nonetheless to the point. In the initial interview, our approach can easily become cold and threatening. Extracting all the necessary statistics of the inquirer's life can have the charm of a jailhouse third degree. And in the maze of the problematic, the question of mystery is often lost: "What are you looking for?"

Raising this question is essential; it is preface for the story. And if we have made no assumptions, if our "noticing" has been hospitable, the question will be non-threatening and will allow whatever answer is comfortable for the inquirers. The primary implication, of course, is that we allow them to *answer* the question. That granted, it is a good probability that, like the potential disciples in the Gospel who responded, "Where are you staying?" the inquirers' first response will be just a feeler for a friendly invitation to "come and see." Here it is crucial that we imitate the wisdom of Jesus, who *resisted the temptation to tell them what they were really looking for*! Instead, he simply gave them a gracious invitation which allowed them time to sort out the deeper questions for themselves. Inquirers need time to raise all the questions: what am I looking for, where am I coming from, where am I going, and what my responsibility is in all of this? These questions are an extended way of saying, "What is my story?"

Among the ministers of initiation, "story" is in danger of becoming a casualty of meaningless jargon. Story as it is used here is not to be confused with the historic recounting of life details. It is the lived-out interpretation of the milestone events of personal history. Story is remembered in my bones, present now in the person I have become as a result of how I have understood these significant events. It is how I name my experience.

Each of us has a story, rooted in the memory of where I have come from, arbitrating my truce with the present, shaping my hope or fear of where I may be going. I must have a story, it is my identity. Without it, I become amnesiac, cut off and alone in a world of relationships. But stories are much like dreams. We all have them; yet, like dreams, we may or may not be aware of them. And even among those who are in touch with their stories, some will know how to interpret them and some will not. Providing the inquirer the opportunity to touch and experience his/her own story is the first step of the precatechumenate: "Where are you staying?"

Come and See

Awareness of one's story is only the beginning. The ultimate goal is to sensitively *interpret* that story and experience in the light of the Gospel. Our story alone is seldom good news. The dynamics of evangelization puts the individual story in dialogue with the Gospel story. "Come and see. See that you are not alone. Come and see where I am staying (in your life)." It is this Gospel dialogue that offers us a new perception of what has already gone on in our lives. It gives us a new story. This new story—the good news—cannot be applied like a topical ointment. To come and see does not offer packaged information, but an opportunity to *discover* the truth for oneself. Like the discovery that birds still sing in the midst of urban uproar, good news is discovered beyond the clatter of information through fine tuning and deeper listening:

> So now when I pray
> I sit and turn my mind
> like a television knob
> till you are there
> with your large, open hands

spreading my life before me
like a Sunday tablecloth
and pulling up a chair yourself
for by now
the secret is out.
You are home
(Shea 90).

This is evangelizing discovery: to find Christ at home.

They Came and Saw

We can only imagine what dialogue, what sharing of dreams went on that evening, as Jesus and these two men became acquainted. What is clear is that they experienced good news. The first thing Andrew did the next day was to find his brother Simon and tell him, "We have found the Messiah! Come and see for yourself!" Just like that they were evangelized! How could that be?

"We have found him." Catechumenal teams and people of God, hear this! Evangelization is not about instruction but about meeting Christ. For the apostles, understanding Jesus came slowly and imperfectly, but the authenticity of his person was immediate. Christ's words carried authority, not because he was in management, but because he was authentic. Because of that, they followed him. It is no different today.

Inviting others to come and see is risky business. We are asking them to lean into our communal life, past the surface images into what lies beyond. "What you see is what you get" is a truism that holds sobering possibilities in initiation. We are not perfect, but we must be authentic. The evangelizing encounter is Christ. We must re-*present* him. Here begins the credibility of Real Presence.

Authentic encounter begets union—they remained with him. The source of that staying power is laying roots of relationship, seeing a connection between Jesus and daily living. The difference between "good news" and simply "news" is its positive significance for me. The human propensity for believing the worst dies hard. It is typified by our common response to good news: "I can't believe it!" Often repeated testimony is needed before the good news sinks in. This is why Christians tell their story, that others may finally make the connection that this news is *their* news, and that it is good.

In the precatechumenate, members of the community tell their faith story, not to present themselves as "experts" in journeying, but to share, to be vulnerable with the inquirers in the risk of storytelling, to be poured out first, and most of all to offer living connection with Christ. Great care must be taken to see that personal faith sharing provides this connective catalyst without which the repetition of faith journeys becomes an exercise in narcissism.

A friend once asked me, "How do we show this connection when sharing our faith journey?" In his encyclical on evangelization, Pope Paul VI proclaims that the "kernel and center" of the Evangel is "liberation from everything that oppresses man[kind]" (Pope Paul VI, *Evangelii Nuntiandi* [1976], 10). The story of liberation is a continuous thread throughout all of Scripture. This scriptural testimony arose out of living tradition; liberation has always been the common experience of those whose lives are pulled into tandem with the God who saves. That tradition and experience is born out in our lives today. The Word is still being spoken. The saving connection is made when those who know their enslavements can share a moment of freedom. It is not a matter of technique but of mentality, of recognizing the way things are: we enslave ourselves; God sets people free. Our model is Jesus. At the beginning of his public life, Christ proclaimed liberty to captives, and then stood up and witnessed of himself that the passage was fulfilled in their hearing! (Lk 4:18).

They Remained with Him

Jesus evangelized by establishing relationships. So do we. The precatechumenate is a time for establishing trust and communication, a time for bonding that speaks to the possibility of common life in Christ (Kavanagh, *Shape*, 129). Deeper communication that issues in relationship is not easy. Inquirers, no less than ourselves, are influenced by the cultural addiction to problem solving, They often skirt the risky personal issues by giving importance to the more manageable, technical questions. With Andrew, they like to ask, "Where are you (Catholics) staying?" Here again, we must follow the example of Jesus. He didn't say, "I am staying down by the lake, third hut on the right" but "Come and see." This was an invitation past the technicalities into the mystery. It is our challenge to do the same. If we are faithful to this challenge, then "churchy" questions should eventually give way to Gospel issues. It is a good indication that the heart of the evangelizing dialogue has not been reached if non-essential questions continue to abound. In the face of such questions, it is important that the catechumenate team respond—not so much answering them but discovering why surface concerns have usurped the primary mission of discerning Christ. I do not suggest that these other questions be ignored, but simply put into perspective. As I see it, the precatechumenate is a time of inquiry, not simply into the by-laws of an organization but into viable answers to the eternal question, "Quo vadis?" ("Where are you going?"). An assumption that the Catholic church is the cut-and-dried answer to the inquirer's question bypasses the primary answer: conversion to *Christ* as the Way. "They remained with *him*." The church is only a vehicle of the

Christ encounter. Rightfully, the traveler needs to know whether this vehicle is a reliable and suitable means of getting there. Therefore, a certain amount of inquiry about the church is appropriate. But the church is not the journey. Perpetual inspection of the bus won't get you down the road. There must come a time when the inquirer identifies the real destination and commits to passage. The inquirer commits to passage in Christ upon entrance into the catechumenate. Many of the Catholic questions that still persist can be answered on an informal basis by the candidate's sponsor. The more difficult doctrinal questions are appropriately handled by a knowledgeable catechist during the catechumenate.

There are those who would suggest that evangelization is only for those who have not yet known Christ, and that therefore the precatechumenate is unnecessary for catechized and practicing Christians approaching from other faiths. If Pope Paul VI and Christ are correct—that Good News is liberation—then why is it that there are so many enslaved and manacled Christians? Might it not suggest that evangelization is neglected in many Christian quarters, or not properly understood, and that therefore the catechizing that occurs often echoes human voicings and not the divine Word that frees? I contend that the fact that people have been catechized does not automatically assure that they have been evangelized. Of course we recognize and honor the ongoing presence and interaction of Christ in the lives of the already baptized. But the very fact that candidates from other Christian faiths present themselves as inquirers signals that they quest for something different or deeper. They have set out on a journey. This implies departure as well as destination. They believe that they are changing churches. They may well be changing Christs and Gods (Dunning). In my view, that involves evangelization as well as conversion.

While we must be sensitive to the fact that their starting point is different from the uncatechized, I believe that we must not deprive them of the opportunity to ask, to discover and to dialogue their story. Remembering that catechesis is the echo of the Word that is heard, it is vital that they have the opportunity to discern whether or not their hearing has been true or impaired. Distortion is an ever-present possibility in the process of human hearing. Eyes that do not see and ears that do not hear are enduring phenomena. From this standpoint, evangelization, like conversion, is an on-going process of life for all of us.

The Jesus Mentality

As we look back at the Gospel narrative, we can see the evangelizing mentality unfold through five modes of behavior: to notice, question, invite, share and connect. It seems maddeningly simple: receptive noticing, raising the right questions, allowing them to see for themselves rather than be told, sharing common journeys, and establishing relationships. In the real world, it doesn't always seem that simple. Nevertheless, I am convinced that if initiation ministers develop and sensitively use these five behavioral patterns they will find the precatechumenal mission greatly simplified, and effectively on target. It really amounts to an attitude, a way of being with people. The difficulty is overcoming the western propensity to be doers, problem solvers, and in charge. Sometimes it calls the team members to conversion of a major magnitude. So be it. The heart of the precatechumenate is prophetic and powerful. In short, our discomfort with evangelization is an honest one, deep down we know the risk: encounter with the Christ in us.

For Discussion

- As a team, what is your posture toward each inquirer who comes?

- How is each inquirer welcomed for whom he or she is on the journey of faith? How is respect for his or her journey prior to coming to you conveyed? In what ways do you respond to these inquirers as co-journeyers with them? How do you find out what they already know about faith; for whom they are looking; for what they are asking?

- How as a team do you lead the inquirers to discover the touch of God in their lives? How do you use the Scripture to help inquirers understand how their story is connected to the story of salvation?

- The dynamics of storytelling involve risk. In what ways do you as team reduce the risk involved? Often, people are invited to tell their story. Is it critical that everyone know every person's story or that every person has the opportunity to share his or her story with one other person so that together the group names the elements of truth and connects these elements to the *big story*— Scripture or stories of salvation history?

The Rite Application

While this Gospel narrative shapes for us a behavior and a mentality in which inquiry and evangelization can flourish, it leaves the signs of victory unnamed. Has evangelization occurred? Are the inquirers ready to move on? How do we know that? When is the connection with the story strong enough to sustain the tug of conversion? In essence, these are questions of content, asking how much and to what degree.

Here we must tussle with the mystery of relationship. It does not easily yield to quantitative concerns. The "how much" of a relationship can only appropriately be measured in terms of its quality. For the catechumenate team, the question is how to help the inquirers discern within themselves the vitality of a budding, rediscovered or redesigned relationship with Jesus Christ, who is their Good News. What and where are the guidelines for that?

Read the Rites

This is not a putdown, any more than "Read Scripture" is a putdown. In all honesty, "Read the rites" is likely to be a fair suggestion, given the American way of doing things. Out of our rugged individualism and can-do determination arises the wry commentary, "When all else fails, read the directions." More frequently than not, it is the last thing we do. But for ministers seeking direction, discernment, and guidelines for the precatechumenate, paragraph 42 will bring clarity. Before inquirers may be accepted into the order of catechumens, the rites enjoin that certain fundamentals of Christian spiritual life be evident in the lives of the candidates. These fundamentals are: first faith, initial conversion, a sense of repentance, the initial practice of prayer, a sense of church, and some experience of the spirit of Christian community. These are loaded phrases. Single words have volumes of meaning packed into them. Like a large software program condensed on a small disc, the contents must be "uncompressed" before they can be utilized.

First Faith

Does "first faith" imply that there can be second, third...and final faith? If so, how can one "keep the faith" if it is constantly evolving? Is first faith the same as basic beliefs? What is faith? These are not idle questions. Similar questions have been raised repeatedly, and many have struggled with the answers. The answers, like initiation itself, are rooted in experience and are owned only little by little. The stages of faith have been explored and expounded by experts, and it is important for those who would guide and facilitate another's search for faith to understand and recognize these stages (cf. Fowler; Stokes). But for our purposes here, what we are looking for is a basic, bottom-line, gut-level understanding that the ministers of initiation themselves bring to the process. That is what they will communicate with every act and word they speak.

What is this faith that makes Christians? Emphatically, it is not a set of once-and-for-all beliefs. Essentially, faith is an orientation of person, a way of leaning into life, a way of evaluating everything about life. It is a filter by which we can perceive God's active presence in all things and beings. Faith is the awareness of and response to this relational Presence in our lives. As in any relationship, faith does not happen all at once, nor is the fullness of it ever possessed. Christian faith is the experience that the incarnation is a reality, that God became human not only for us but in us.

Understood in this context, the concept of "first faith" makes sense (awareness of Presence grows), "keeping faith" is made possible (fidelity in relationship), and basic Christian belief can finally be understood as incarnational (who, not what). Such a definition of faith may be easily assented to intellectually but not so easily incorporated in deeper understanding. Language betrays our faith understanding. Compare the common phraseologies: "I believe on the Lord Jesus" (Jesus as object, a possessable commodity); "I believe in the Lord Jesus" (Jesus as concept, an intellectual premise); "I believe you, Lord Jesus" (Jesus as person, a transforming presence). In his song-credo, "You In Our Day," composer Rory Cooney captures this bottom-line, incarnational faith:

> We have not seen you, but we love you.
> We have not seen you, but we believe you.
> We have not seen you, but we hope in you.
> For we have met you in our day.
> We have met you on the way
>
> (© 1987, North American Liturgy Resources (NALR),
> 5536 NE Hassalo, Portland, OR 97213. All rights reserved.
> Used with permission).

What is called for in the rites by first faith is not a question of what (the rules, the dogmas, the church structure) but of Who. First faith is the primal recognition that the incarnating

God is found in flesh and blood; the divine is met in the human. As ministers, we ourselves must be clear about that.

Initial Conversion

An incarnational faith transforms our life-doing. This first redoing of life is called initial conversion. In a sense, conversion is *always* initial in that transformation is self-defined as "forming over," a re-creation, a new birth. To be always at the beginning is a significant component in the understanding of conversion as a life process. It also precludes a smug, consumeristic "I have it, you don't" attitude about the faith and conversion.

Words like love, faith, conversion, and prayer are often watered down or deformed in common usage as they are fitted into our cultural comfort-zone. The term "conversion" is commonly misused, especially in the bulk of televangelism, to mean a one-on-one private happening between myself and Jesus in which I agree to keep all the rules and he agrees to take charge of my life and grant in-house benefits. Such a tit-for-tat, private bargaining table agreement between God and myself cannot be farther from the biblical concept of conversion.

Though not formally dogmatized in Scripture, it is clear that from Genesis to Acts the single-minded understanding of conversion is a returning to *covenant* (Dick 43). Although "covenant" is a complex and layered concept, the covenant with Yahweh in the Old and New Testaments was never understood as a bilateral contract between equals; rather, it was understood as a "disposition" of God by which God declared and instituted a relationship of fidelity between God and God's people so binding as to be called *hesed*, the Hebrew word signifying the loyalty and affection of blood kinsmen (McBrien 914; *Theological Dictionary* vol. 2, 114, 134). Thus, "I will be your God and you shall be my people" declared a fidelity of kinship, of blood brotherhood as it were, between Yahweh and his people, Israel. It was a covenant of mutual fidelity in *community*. The testimony to this unbreakable bond between God and God's people was the Ten Commandments, the focus of which is almost entirely communal integrity. For covenant there must be a faithful people, even if only a remnant. In Scripture, the call to conversion was a call for Israel to return in fidelity to the God-covenant which gave it birth, to re-examine itself and its responsibilities to be a holy nation. Conversion today can be no less. It calls us also to a re-envisoning of covenant, the pact of a faithful people to a New Covenant in his blood. We are called to the mutual gifting of God-life to one another in community, to return to the fidelity of blood brotherhood. It is called seeking the kingdom.

To make sense out of the rites, we must understand conversion in this biblical way. Holding firmly in mind that conversion is returning to covenant fidelity (a whole people acting together in relationship with God), the language of the rites unpacks in a new way. It becomes clear why the entire process must take place *in the midst of a community* and why it calls both the inquirer and the inviting community to examine together the implications of paschal living, of dying and rising in a common life in Christ. Within the mentality of Scripture, conversion cannot happen outside the context of community.

As we have already seen, the mechanism that sets up this relationship of life to life is dialoguing their stories with The Story. At the celebration of Passover, the story of the liberating and faithful God of Israel is always told, how God led God's people out of slavery, across the desert of trial, and into a place of freedom and new life. Yahweh's faithfulness calls forth a faithful people who will in turn keep covenant with their God.

In this we see the connection between storytelling and doctrine. In the storytelling we hear how God acts and who God is in the midst of God's people throughout all of history;

out of this arises the truths about God that we can rely upon and what the terms are of the covenant between this faithful God and God's people. We can also see the connection between evangelizing and conversion. The Good News is not simply that Jesus is my savior, but that if God so loved the world that God gave God's son for its redemption, then we, for our part, must give ourselves for each other. Fidelity calls forth fidelity.

What then, is initial conversion for the inquirer? We see it demonstrated by the thief who, touched by the presence of Jesus, uttered a simple desire: "Lord, remember me when you come into your kingdom." He saw the goodness of Jesus and wanted to be near, to follow. But knowing the evil in his own life, he asked only to be remembered. Initial conversion is like pressing one's nose against the glass; it is a movement of desire to share a vision and a life yet beyond one's experience. Initial conversion is the hope and growing expectation of re-membrance, of becoming united with the members of the One who gives life, and the willingness to re-form one's life accordingly.

A Sense of Repentance

Repentance dawns with the rising recognition that we have broken covenant, that our egotism, privatism, consumerism, militarism, and all the other "isms" have pre-empted the promise to be gift for one another. Repentance is the preface to conversion as it comes to grips with the parts of my personal story that hang in limbo, estranged from Other, distanced from the saving and transforming presence of God in Christ. As those moments of alienation are brought into the focus of God who keeps covenant, the brokenness comes to light; wholeness and unity beckon, not in and of oneself but with and for others. Remorse for having behaved badly without the understood need of reconciliation is not Christian repentance.

A sense of repentance must necessarily involve reconciliation and harmony with others. In the Gospel, the invitation to repent was always followed by the reminder that the kingdom is near.

The Practice of Prayer

It is to be noted that the rite speaks of prayer in the singular. The practice enjoined is not the multiplication of exercises extraneous to oneself, as in saying prayers, but rather an abiding mentality, a state of being, an approach to life. Like faith, prayer is a quality of the person, not a conformity to a system of exercises or beliefs. Initiation ministers must understand that merely leading the inquirers in the saying of prayers does not *per se* form anyone in the practice of prayer. Rather, prayer, like faith, is encouraged by shared experience and example of a prayerful life-style. In essence, prayer and faith are two sides of the same coin, the core of which is the awareness of and the response to the living presence of God. If prayer is understood as divine-human encounter, then it is, in fact, the heart of the precatechumenate. But how often is the saying of prayers substituted for the experience of prayer? Is the inquirers' opportunity to practice prayer limited to listening to somebody else's prayers—prayers that, more often than not, are self-conscious, rote offerings? What understanding of prayer does the facilitator of these sessions have and transmit by these recitations? Does such an understanding encourage the true practice of prayer? Moreover, if the facilitator does all the praying, what does this say to the inquirers? Can they really believe that they have been gifted with good news, calling forth thanksgiving and love? Can they believe that they have anything to give to this community, this body of members who must say to each other, "I have great need of you"?

Prayer arises out of a sense of presence and interconnectedness; it is aspiration, a shared life-breath. It is being in the presence of the Other. As such, prayer (whether spoken aloud or held in the heart) happens spontaneously in a group in which gifts are truly shared and honored, and in which covenant (mutual fidelity) is kept. A facilitator who honors the Spirit present within all persons will evoke from the group a spontaneous sense of praise and thanksgiving to the God who made all things well. The spirit of prayer is a trustworthy barometer of the health of the whole catechumenal process. The spirit and the practice of prayer is intrinsically linked to the "experience of the society and spirit of Christians."

A Sense of Church

The one great doctrine of the Catholic church that should be central in the precatechumenate is the *nature* of the church, which is the corporate Christ, now here present. The wonderful imaging of Scripture presents this reality in terms of vine and branches, and of a wholesome body made of many members, unified by a single life and a single purpose. An important understanding common to both images is that the life of Christ is had in common, that to sustain life, we must stay connected to the source, and that what affects one member affects the whole. Without this sense of church, dialoguing one's personal story with the Gospel tends to remain in idealistic ether rather than incarnated in a transforming reality.

This corporate sense of church stands over against a common mentality that salvation is a private affair, a matter of one's individual perfection. As Americans, that individualistic mentality is an insidious part of our culture. As ministers of the Rite of Christian Initiation of Adults, we must constantly be on guard against the seduction of private salvation. We teach ecclesiology much more by example than by instruction. During this period when the inquirers are challenged to discover the dwelling place of Christ today, it is vital that we offer an authentic model of the corporate Christ (the mystical body), testifying with our lives that when one member is afflicted, the rest offer help and stamina, and that the hand cannot say to the foot, "I have no need of you." Accepting a corporate ecclesiology will be for many the most radical form of changing churches. It means that to choose Christian faith is to choose a living and membered Christ, members that are human and as yet imperfect; that therefore the church itself is not perfect but a *becoming* entity. Many would prefer to have a church that is boxed and possessed, an inanimate commodity that requires nothing except to be owned. The truth is otherwise. The church is not a commodity to be possessed but a relationship to be cherished and developed.

Christian Society

The catechetical content for the precatechumenate is plainly stated: first faith, conversion, repentance, prayer, church and Christian society. What should also be clear by now is that these elements do not fit cleanly into any curriculum as items to be taught. They are in fact, life issues, experiences that can be transmitted only by shared living. Therefore, the presumption is that the inquirers are put into contact with real Christian households in which these experiences are the givens, and in which hospitality (as in sensitive noticing) is natural. God forbid that the precatechumenal process be relegated to the cold and unwelcoming walls of the church classroom! A much more nurturing, affirming, and personal environment must be provided, at least in the early stages. A Christian home creatively provides an atmosphere naturally attuned to the work of this period.

In the home, groups are limited to an intimate size conducive to personal sharing and honest questioning. In this small intimate group it is much easier for the *inquirers* to set the agenda; whereas the classroom atmosphere inescapably suggests that the agenda belongs to the "teacher," the team leader. Small core groups learn how to listen to each other, care for one another, support one another; it is an in-the-nutshell experience of the society and spirit of Christians. In the course of mutual sharing, they learn to pray *together*. These are some of the natural advantages of using homes.

A home-based precatechumenate also keeps us more honest. The catechumenate team does not appear as the experts who have all the answers but as representative members of the engendering community *whose authenticity is held in common.* This family-style community sets aright the pernicious inclination to initiate people into an "initiation reception committee" instead of into the living and breathing parish community. And finally, it requires of the catechumenate team members themselves commitment to a real trust walk (which they so often like to impose on the candidates). Unable to see what is going on in every home, they must trust in the Spirit of God at work within the individuals and families of their parish. That does not mean indiscriminate abandon. Careful discernment and a great deal of care and prayer should go into the selection and training of these families. It means that those selected must themselves be people of prayer, open to the divine encounter. But that said and done, the team leaders must then relinquish proprietorship with the healthy realization that conversion and faith are not the work of humans but of the divine Initiator.

A number of parishes throughout the country can bear witness to the effectiveness of holding the precatechumenate in selected parish homes. Perhaps the greatest relief this plan offers the catechumenate team is that an ongoing pre-catechumenate is always available, and the time frame for the inquirers is totally flexible. That advantage alone should offer enticement to overburdened teams who have been operating under a nine-month process that makes no precatechumenal provision for the latecomer or those not ready to move on to the catechumenate. Humanly, change is often shunned in favor of familiar pain; control preferred over creativity. But the bottom line is this: how can the evangelizing dialogue best be served? All in all, an at-home environment puts inquiry and evangelization within "do-able" reach. It brings the mystery of the other into approachable range where stories can be heard and told. (And it's the way Jesus did it!)

I do not suggest that the whole inquiry period be limited to small group meetings. On the contrary, I would insist that the entire group get together in a festive manner several times during the course of the precatechumenate. These would be social gatherings, times to get to know the broader group, to share insights, joys, fears, comic situations, whatever is part of their journey. As the time of the Rite of Acceptance approaches, this kind of gathering could also provide opportunity for group preparation for the rites.

The core community structure does not, of course, eliminate the need for initial private interviews with the candidates. The purpose of the interview is to discern individual needs, attitudes and background, and to uncover any special situations requiring timely attention. Properly and sensitively done, these interviews are indispensable. Likewise, follow-up interviews during the catechumenate and during Lent offer the candidate a sense of guidance and aid immensely in the process of discernment at the time of election.

Discerning Readiness: Putting It All Together

The language that pops right out of paragraph 42 is the repeated use of "first" and "initial" as applied to the required formation. The rites make it abundantly clear that the church recognizes conversion as on on-going process, that this is indeed only the beginning. The hope of the precatechumenate is that within the inquirers, the seeds of faith, conversion, repentance, prayer, and a sense of church and Christian society are planted, fed, and given plenty of growing room. What is expected of the inquirers is not harvest but that the seed break soil and show signs of growth. At this stage of the process, the spiritual fundamentals named are not so much areas of judgment as they are arenas of development. In this sense, paragraph 42 of the rites addresses not only the inquirers' readiness to move on but also delineates the team members' responsibilities to provide experiences which can evoke such development in the precatechumens. The measuring is mutual. The discernment is shared.

The whole period of the precatechumenate has been given over to the inquirer as a time for questioning. Now the time has come for the first response. The director assists the individual to discern his or her own true inner desire: does this person truly wish to publicly commit to the catechumenal life? That is the basic discernment: whether or not the individual has the inner desire to make such a commitment in the midst of the community. The decision is therefore largely up to the inquirer who alone knows knows his or her inner motivation. Nevertheless, an unexamined or shallow choice is to be avoided. The fruits of initial faith, conversion, prayer etc. are named by the rite as external indicators of the interior journey. These solid beginnings are vital to an honest commitment to the rigors of the catechumenate. For the sake of the candidate, the director should not hesitate to challenge an obviously shallow motivation. In cases of uncertainty however, the inquirer is always given the benefit of the doubt. In essence, the invitation to "come and see" is only retracted if the individual is simply not willing to come along, or to open to the journey.

If, however, an inquirer discerns unreadiness for himself or herself, initiation ministers ought not interpret that as failure on their part, as if each conversion was the product of the team's endeavor. They can plant and water, but only God gives the harvest. Besides, inquiry means exactly that; "browsers" are welcome. The hospitable response to unreadiness is to offer any viable assistance for discerning the next step, while fully respecting the individual's freedom.

The question of the precatechumenate has been, "Master, where do you dwell?" Having pressed one's nose against the glass, and raised all manner of questions about the life within view, it is time to lean through, time to enter in. The invitation is extended.

R.S.V.P.

For Discussion

- What are the prerequisites for the first step, Rite of Acceptance? Read RCIA paragraph 42. As a team, determine in what ways these prerequisites are integrated into your precatechumenate period. This dialogue gives you, the team, an excellent understanding of discernment and all that it implies. Discernment is with each inquirer and the team; it is not a discernment of the group's readiness to move on in the process. This demands that the team be ready or in the process of being stretched to an on-going process in order to meet the needs of the inquirers who come knocking at the doors of the parish. It also demands that the team discern the needs of each person because some inquirers come with a Christian faith and are seeking full communion with us while others come with no knowledge or relationship with God or Jesus Christ. Do you treat them all the same? Refer to RCIA Part II, chapters 4 and 5.

The Rite Mentality

All true rituals are memory-makers and memory-shakers. Good ritual is how we remember who we are and celebrate who we shall become. It is how we name our experience and how we revitalize, intensify, and extend that experience to bring integrity and continuity to our lives. One of the great powers of Catholicism is its ritual life, its sacramentality. Those who leave the church may castigate her, but rarely can they forget her. It is the ritual they remember, and it is by ritual that they re-member again with her.

Human belonging in any relational group always seeks ritualization. Initiation rituals abound in human history from primitive times to the present. But ritual is even more pervasive than that; humans routinely ritualize not just initiation, but other significant moments of passage. Rituals of love and hate, peace and war, arrival and departure, birth and death, membering and ids-membering are the warp and woof of human identity. Religions which choose to ignore this do so at their own peril. The de-sacrament sacramental of evangelical and fundamental protestantism has contributed to continual fractionating and individualism, and the loss of rottenness and deep identity among its members. Ritual re-plays and re-pairs our fundamental *connected*; it is the symbolic activity that transcends self-boundary through a timeless identity with others and with the Wholly Other. The implications for initiation are enormous. Without this sacramental sense of life expressed in ritual, the process can become one-dimensional, a jigsaw puzzle enterprise. Evangelizing can easily reduce to proselytizing, and conversion can collapse into moral. We Catholics must beware. We are inclined to squander the ritual treasure that we have by trivializing and/or mechanizing it.

In an address given at the Forum Convocation in September 1987 (Washington, DC), Aidan Kavanagh gave the Rite of Christian Initiation of Adults less than a fifty-fifty chance of survival unless its ministers recognize and allow initiation to be what it is: the *rite of Christian initiation.* The whole thing is a rite—not just the special liturgical rituals that mark crucial moments of passage but the whole process, from pre-catechumenate to mystagogia. In true ritual fashion, initiation is constantly recalling the story and re-entering the experience in order to bring present reality to wholeness and continuity. Its ritual nature roots initiation not only in the mutuality of Christian experience but in the transcendence of it. Without this opportunity to transcend oneself, transformation is impossible and the whole conversion endeavor reverts to a project of problem-solving: that one-dimensional, jigsaw-puzzle mentality. We need to recover the fundamental sense of ritual and symbol which will help us reclaim a sacramental experience of time and enable us to celebrate our deep connectedness to one another and all of creation. True Christian ritual is a remedy for rampant individualism; at the same time it saves all our sacraments from magical manipulation of things because ritual is essentially interpersonal.

The Rite of Acceptance into the Catechumenate

"What is your name?" Who are you? For a long time the precatechumens have struggled with that question, trying to discover their story and seeking ties with the Other Story. It is all ritualized in the opening dialogue of the Rite of Acceptance into the Order of Catechumens: Who are you? What do you ask? Where will that lead? In a sense, their past, present and future are all brought together in a timeless moment. At least it can be, if the precatechumenate has really been faithful to these questions and if the presider himself buys into ritual.

This requires that the presider himself be a man of deep memory who savors the riches of life and who knows how to celebrate them. Unfortunately, some presbyters seem more concerned with the length of the Mass than with the celebration of life before them. In the "interest of time," names are rattled off without any sense of identity or omitted all together, and the ensuing dialogue is no dialogue at all, but an exercise in rote. (God forbid that the presider should have to *talk* to each one of them, and then allow each one to *answer*. What a waste of time!) This attitude is a hold-over from sacramental minimalism: get the right matter and form, say the words, perform the action, stand back and watch it work. However, Vatican II has declared that the *doing* of the work *(ex opere operantis)* is equally as important as the *work done (ex opere operato)*. The Council recalls us to the reality that life is changed not just by what we do, but *how* we do it. "Good celebrations foster and nourish faith. Poor celebrations may weaken and destroy it" is warning for all ritual, whether sacrament or sacramental *(Music in Catholic Worship* 6). But giving up minimalism has its risks. The Rite of Christian Initiation of Adults is so immersed in the reality of the conversion journey that if the presider is caught up in the *doing* of the rites at all, he will inexorably be exposed to the experience of his own internal pilgrimage and the question of

41

its authenticity. Dialogue, even ritual dialogue, can be a risky and sometimes draining enterprise. It measures a man.

The signation of the senses is perhaps the most deeply moving of all the rites outside of the Easter sacraments. The cruciform is traced eight times on the flesh of the candidate, summarized in a ninth all-inclusive sign of the cross. By this sign, more than by any words, we define Christian discipleship, announce the meaning of baptism, and delineate the path of the Christian journey. It situates our journey in the way of the Incarnate One, consecrating our whole bodily entity to crucifixion, to death and to resurrection in Christ. In the power of this rite, the dangerous memory of the cross has been etched on the present moment. It is the mark of each day's passage in Christ.

For Discussion

- In light of the dialogue thus far, name the ways in which you have been affirmed in your catechumenal ministry.

- Name the ways in which you have been challenged to stretch your catechumenal ministry.

- In the period of the precatechumenate, what do you need to keep doing? What do you need to stop doing? How are you going to bring about the change?

- What do you as a team understand to be the "precatechumenate mentality"?

- What can you do to disseminate this information to the parish?

Part Two

The Catechumenal Mentality

"Leaning through the looking glass:
risking the adventure"

FOCAL ISSUES: journey and conversion

What Is the Catechumenal Mentality?

When evening had come, he said to them, "Let us go
across to the other side." And leaving the crowd behind,
they took him with them in the boat, just as he was....A
great windstorm arose, and the waves beat into the boat,
so that the boat was already being swamped. But he was
in the stern, asleep on the cushion; and they woke him
up and said to him, "Teacher, do you not care that we
are perishing?" He woke up and rebuked the wind, and
said to the sea: "Peace! Be still!" Then the wind ceased,
and there was a dead calm. He said to them, "Why are
you afraid? Have you still no faith?" And they were filled
with great awe and said to one another, "Who then is
this, that even the wind and the sea obey him?"
(Mk 4:35-41).

In the jargon of initiation, the ideas of the "farther shore"
and "crossing over" translate into *journey* and *conversion*. In
the period of the catechumenate, these two concepts are
primary issues. The journey to faith begins in earnest for the
catechumen, a trip oftentimes fraught with unexpected and
frightening squalls: issues of conversion that seem overpower-

ing. Cresting these testy waves doubles and triples the distance of the crossing. Passage to the "farther shore" is farther than one would first imagine. The early church knew this, anticipating anywhere from three years to a life-time for catechumens to find courage enough in the midst of life's storms to ask, "Who can this be?"

Today the church still reminds us that it may take years for the catechumenal process to bear the desired fruit, and the National Statutes for the American church call for nothing less than a full year for the catechumenal period (RCIA 6, 76). Nevertheless, catechumenate teams are often embarrassed and irritated by this long timeframe. We are embarrassed because most of us slipped into the church as infants without raising so much as a ripple in the sea of life. (Nobody asked such conversion, such transformation of us!) And we are irritated because our American bias is for instantaneous, visible results. (Can we ask them to wait that long?) In reality, of course, Christian discipleship has always been a call to conversion whether or not we personally have heard it well. And the issue in conversion is not church membership, but the passage through death into life. These are not momentary issues, but those which define life itself. This journey is not a walk across the street into a church door, and this conversion is not a simple switch-over like putting an adaptor on a motor so that it can run on different fuel. The rite is talking epic journey and essential transformation.

The fact that the rite says this plainly and that the fact has been reiterated by every piece of commentary on the rite since its inception has not restrained many from persisting in a program of information and graduation. We need to wrestle with this attitude. It is a pernicious trivializing of the Gospel; it smells of clericalism. A "clerk" is one charged with the care of records and information. The cleric's job is a maintenance, preservation and control operation. The dictionary defines clericalism as the principle or policy of clerical control.

Authoritative information is the issue; being right is the payoff. In the end, clericalism seeks social and political control; in its ignorance, it presumes that knowledge can give life. *Wrong.* It was wrong for Adam with his tree of knowledge of good and evil; wrong for the Pharisees who kept every jot and tittle of the Law; wrong for a church whose mission is Christ, the crucified and living One. In Christian initiation, the issue is not information but living. Dangerous living.

Such living develops only when one perceives journey and conversion as more than separate pieces of this process. Initiation ministry is schizophrenic without understanding the *coincidental nature* of these two elements. By "coincidental" I do not mean "accidental." I mean their exact correspondence in space and in time. One doesn't happen without the other. Although conceptually discreet, journey and conversion are experientially concurrent. We don't "turn around" (conversion) without directional movement or thrust (journey). If pastors and catechumenate team members are not experiencing ongoing conversion themselves, they will perceive journey and conversion as separate, imagining that the major task of the journey is to captain the ship to the other shore and to give our travelers safe passage, as if conversion would happen on arrival. The church clearly challenges this mentality:

> The time spent in the catechumenate should be long enough—several years if necessary—for the *conversion* and *faith* of the catechumens to become *strong*. By their *formation in the entire Christian life* and a *sufficiently prolonged* probation the catechumens are properly initiated into the *mysteries* of salvation...they are *led into the life* of faith, worship, and charity... (RCIA 76, my emphasis).

From this it is clear that the issue is not arrival, but passage. Although it is more comforting for us disciples to think that we climb into the boat in order to get to the other shore,

Christ historically and ecclesially knows that the crux of the journey is *what happens on the way.*

"How," we might ask, "does one go about taking a journey whose destination is the trip itself?" It sounds like the paradoxical *koan*: "What is the sound of one hand clapping?" Direct encounter with mystery is foreign to western thinking; we don't like to deal with open-ended issues. Yet here it is before us: if the purpose of the journey is the process of crossing over, then the point of destination is mainly there to give orientation to the real business of passage. Conversion does not come at the end of the journey as in arrival (when does one ever arrive?) but within the journey as in *paschal mystery.* Failure to come to terms with this coincidence of journey and conversion is what creates the monster of an inquiry class dropped into the initiation framework using unrelated rites to break up the monotony of it all. It becomes a project of arrival.

There is nothing from Exodus to Calvary to support an "arrival" mentality. The reason the Israelites took forty years to cross the desert wasn't because the desert was that big but because their heads and hearts were that hard. Obviously, Yahweh was concerned about passage, not arrival. And when arrival finally came, it was really the beginning of another passage into the Promised Land. And the beat went on—from captivity to freedom, from calvary to resurrection, from fear to pentecost—and now the passage is ours. The elder, the presbyter of the people must above all others understand the story and the passage. Nevertheless, it is oftentimes the presbyter who insists on looking for signs of arrival (where's the completed package of information that signals the end of the course?). Better it is that we take our cue from Christ: book passage with them, take the trip, embrace the storm.

For Discussion

- What are you presently doing during the catechumenate period? When does it begin? What are the elements that belong to this period?

- What do you understand by the term "conversion"? Would you describe your process to be more informational or formational? Explain.

- In light of your own faith journey, where are you? For anyone involved in the catechumenal process, it is critical that he or she spend time reflecting on his or her faith journey. Conversion is never over until a person crosses the final threshold—death. All of life is either a turning toward God or away from God.

- Read *Conversion and the Catechumenate*, edited by Robert Duggan (New York: Paulist, 1984).

- Read *Rite of Christian Initiation of Adults* paragraphs 75-80. Also read in Appendix III the "Decree on the Church's Missionary Activity *Ad gentes*," nos. 13 and 14. How do these paragraphs support what you are presently doing? How do they challenge?

The Jesus Approach

How does Jesus handle this business of transition from fear to faith, this turn-around of trust we call conversion? Any number of stories from the Gospel narrative can cue us to the attitude of Jesus about faith journey. But in the case of ministering with those who are in the midst of both spiritual and physical transitioning, the storm on the lake seems to be a most apt model. We see Jesus proposing that he and the disciples leave the crowd and cross over to the other side, to which they readily agree. Leaving it up to them to negotiate the boat, Jesus awaits passage with serenity. In fact, he sleeps like a baby. Life-threatening storms arise to batter the travelers, and fear rises in their throats. They cry out, "Don't you care?" Jesus, there through it all, awakens, and with incredible nonchalance, calms the raging elements as well as the shaking disciples. Then, even more incredibly, Jesus wonders why they are filled with terror instead of faith. It was an awe-full moment!! They keep asking, fearful to speak the answer: "Who can this be...?"

Let Us Go Across

There is no doubt about it. This "going across" business is definitely Jesus' idea. Who wants to go to Gerasa? The crowd *here* is appreciative, it's getting late, and storm clouds are building up in the darkening sky. Frankly, we'd rather stay right where we're at. But Jesus says, "Let's cross over to the other side." It takes a fair amount of love and trust to readily agree to an apparently pointless and ill-timed idea. The selling point is that Jesus says let *us* cross over. He's already in the boat; being with him is worth risking the trip.

Let's be honest. How effective can initiation be if the invitation is "Why don't *you* cross over?" "Why don't *you* be converted?" ("I'm just the booking agent.") Generally we are not so blatant about it, since most of us suffer some embarrassment asking others to do what we ourselves will not do. Nevertheless, our invitation often enough is not self-inclusive. The way we overcome that embarrassment is to cling to the conviction that we have already made the trip. (We've arrived.) Oh, we talk a good line. We use the language of mutual journeying and convince ourselves that we're doing it. But if we're honest we can catch our bodies as well as our tongues talking a different language. We image separateness and speak the language of the "arrived" by posturing the teacher and the guru in discussion groups; by transmitting information as from top to bottom; by rephrasing their visions and values into our own perceptions. When "they" learn to parrot our vision in our words and our way, then they too have arrived. It's a big trap for initiation ministers. This business of crossing over has to be a joint venture. Like Jesus, we cross over with the others in the boat *we were already sitting in*!

Leaving the Crowd

Once we finally accept the fact that we who follow Christ are all in the same boat, it eventually dawns on us that it is a very small boat! It's definitely no Queen Mary. A large majority of people would prefer to sit this trip out, thank you. It's a matter of statistics that, all totaled, Christians only comprise about thirty-three percent of the world population. The passage to conversion is not a crowd-pleasing sell-out. This is a tough one for us to swallow. The American measure of success is Big Numbers. Nevertheless, this conversion to the way of the crucified One is not your run-of-the-mill band wagon. In fact, it is undeniably counter-cultural.

If our catechumens and candidates don't begin to feel some distancing from their culture and their society; if they don't ever feel some discomfort in passage, maybe we are only offering a pleasure cruise. An instruction-class model which offers only information and not journey for transformation is like booking passage on the Queen Mary. All the work is done for you, and the whole idea is to make you *feel good*. As a pampered customer, you have a false sense of power and control, of "having it made." And the general mentality of a luxury liner is based on a round trip ticket: a lovely fantasy that brings you right back to where you started.

Christian conversion is more like the passage of the Vietnamese boat people. You set out for an unseen land, there is no turning back, and it is a life-death enterprise. But for us, Jesus is in the back of the boat.

They Took Him with Them in the Boat, Just As He Was

Who is doing what to whom? In Jesus' catechumenate, the catechumens climb into his boat and set out for his choice of port, but they are the sailors. Leaving *them* to negotiate the passage, Jesus goes quietly to the stern.

I hope the parallel is obvious. This is not a top-to-bottom directed operation. "They take him." The mentality is not disinterest on the part of Jesus but of trust. Trust in what? Their ability to keep themselves out of difficulty? Apparently not. Jesus trusted the process. He trusted that if they were allowed to do their own sailing they would eventually confront the real issues of life and salvation: that we are needful, that God gifts those who admit that they are in need, and it is Jesus who saves. Allowing them to "captain their own ship" gave them the opportunity to voluntarily relinquish leadership to Christ. "They took *him*"—it became *their* choice.

Jesus also knows that "doing it all" for his disciples is, in fact, doing nothing for them. It is in the struggle that faith evolves. We need to humbly follow his example: share the boat, set the course, and get out of the way.

A Great Windstorm Arose

Squalls happen.

Squalls are squallier in a small boat; one must immediately come to terms with the water. The power of the water that reveals who we are and who Christ is has obvious baptismal overtones. Water is not only life-giving but death-dealing. St. Paul gave clear warning that baptism into Christ Jesus is baptism into death for the sake of resurrection with him into new life (Rom 6:3). The catechumenate must not gloss over this. We find God in the midst of storms.

Not only do squalls happen, but they seem to be necessary to push us past idolatrous self-reliance. On glassy water, we tend to see our own reflection and to rely on our own power. Let it be noted that Jesus was in no hurry to relieve his disciples' discomfort. "Waves beat into the boat, so that the boat was already being swamped"! He was with them all the time and readily available, but he waited for them to ask for help. A human psychological fact is that help is not helpful until the one in need perceives himself to be needful. Jesus is the Messiah, but he doesn't have a Messiah complex. He allows them to come to him for salvation; he doesn't foist it upon them, ready or not. He trusts the process. Likewise, we must not be disturbed when our catechumens and candidates experience the storms of passage. More importantly, we must remember that we are not saviors. We're companions in passage, sharing the same boat, fighting the same storms. We can help by leaning into the oars or by swinging the boom of the sail, but only Jesus can calm the waters.

Don't You Care? The Boat's Going Down!

This cracks me up. Mark's version of the episode is so much more human than Matthew's. The disciples are frantically trying to stay afloat, and Jesus sleeps through it all. They could have awakened him a lot sooner, but with typical human bull-headedness, they're determined to go it alone. When they can't handle it, they relieve the pressure of failure by finding fault with him, suggesting (respectfully) that Jesus doesn't care. It makes me want to shout, "Of course he cares. He's in the same boat, dummy!"

We forget that. We know it in our heads, but our guts won't buy into incarnation as the poignant reality of God being in the same boat with us. As disoriented creatures, our incredibly self-centered bias sure shows up in times of stress. We not only forget that others share the same liabilities, the same pain; we stubbornly shut them out. We think our situation is unique. When we begin to suspect we're over our heads, we are afraid nobody cares. It's a common human syndrome. It will happen to your catechumens; you can bank on your own anxiety as well. Let's be honest. If you never experience any of this in your catechumenate, in yourself or in others, what you're doing probably has little to do with conversion. This business of conversion has life-death overtones. It can cause fear to rise in our throats; sometimes it pushes us to our limits. We think it's our private Titanic.

The good news is that Jesus is in the same boat, and any time we want to quit trying to save ourselves and everybody else, we can seek his presence. The place to look is in the back of the boat. There are a couple of profound lessons here for initiation ministers. First, the real Messiah doesn't run around trying to save people from the scary stuff of living and dying. Second, conversion happens when we stop bailing water and acknowledge that without Christ, we're dead.

That's the bottom line. We spend a lot of time worrying about the proper application of lessons and doctrine in the catechumenate. As valuable as that is, none of it converts. The telling issue is the relinquishment of life into the hands of Christ. Does he care? Of course he cares. He's in the same boat, dummy. But it is up to us to remember the extraordinary power of the sleeping Christ in our midst—in the back of the boat.

Be Still!

One word from Jesus and the storm is over. That's a great story, we say, but it doesn't work like that now. True. It didn't exactly work that way then, either. It was only after the disciples *invited Jesus into the situation* that it worked that way. Relinquishment is the key. I can personally attest to the fact that it still works that way. Undoubtedly there are many others who can also attest to the incredible calm that ensues when we (for the "umpteenth time") get ourselves out of the god business and let God be God. All the problems aren't solved; we still have to ply the oars to get shore, but we do so in peace born out of the experience of God's presence. God *is* in the same boat, and God's presence is awesome.

What has this to do with ministering in the catechumenate? If your experience with the catechumenate is anything like mine, you will agree that it brings out the messiah complex in all of us. It's really fertile ground for would-be-messiahs, and that's probably most of us in church ministry. We see the folks coming with expectation in their eyes; we may not be expert saviors, but somehow we'll manage. We're not pelagians for nothing! Pelagianism is like the common cold: it is an ailment of vague origin, universal occurrence and undetermined cure. It was first packaged and promulgated by none other than Pelagius, a monk of the late fourth/early fifth century. He rejected the idea that salvation is pure gift, and insisted that man could, with the use of his free will, effect his own salvation by good works (and presumably show others how to do the same). He rejected the universal disorientation of Original Sin. Although condemned as a heretic, Pelagius had a lot of support for his position. Understandably so. The idea has been popular since the Garden of Eden. Like Adam and Eve, he and we want to be do-it-yourself gods, in control of things, including our own and others' salvation. We all have a little pelagianism in us. It got Adam and Eve in big trouble, and it is still big trouble today.

When it comes to deadly stuff like this, Jesus doesn't just model behavior for us. He stands right up and spells it out, "Be still!" It is highly reminiscent of Psalm 46, which is more explicit: "Be still, and know that I am God!" The disciples got the point. In the power of that stillness, they didn't ask, "How did he do that?" Instead they wondered, "Who can this be?"

We would much rather know how he did it! (We'd be on our way to being full-fledged "messiahs" if we could figure that out.) There is some serious truth in this. There is an enormous amount of time and energy spent in religious circles trying to prove we know how to "do it"; each faction trying to prove the other's "how to" is wrong. All of which is beside the point. Conversion happens when humans get beyond themselves into the person of Christ. Priests and catechumenate team members whose body or verbal language says "Watch me. See how I do it, hear how I say it" are obviously more concerned with self-proclamation, showing off their acquired how-to skills. Unfortunately the catechumens will begin to wonder, "Who is this?" but it will not be asked with awe.

The catechumenate can use a lot more quiet than we generally offer, stillness in the presence of him whom the wind and sea obey.

Why Are You Afraid?

In a single breath Jesus linked terror with lack of faith. We are accustomed to the other way of putting it, that perfect love casts out fear. But the word "love" carries a lot of emotional baggage; the word "faith" gives us a clearer shot at the real issue here. In Part One of this book, faith was described as the awareness of and response to God's presence in our lives. A person of faith perceives God as present. It's easy to see why faith and fear are mutually exclusive; if God is with us, who can be against us? That speaks volumes to all of us. Is there anyone among us who is without fear? The cure for fear is not the mustering of courage nor pretence that the boat isn't shipping water. The cure is to seek the presence of Christ. That's faith. The Gospel keeps coming back to that. So must we.

Since the catechumenate is a *faith* journey, terror is something to watch out for. As initiation ministers we need to recognize fear in the catechumens and candidates. Of course true discernment begins with self, dragging out the ghosts in our own closets, recognizing our own fears. Terror can exhibit itself in different ways. Aside from overt shaking, crying and running away, fear can also disguise itself with unlikely masks. Pollyannaism (everything is beautiful), "strong" silence, shallowness, perpetual clowning, intellectualism and having always to be right are some of the ways that humans hide from acknowledged or unacknowledged fear. These can be signals that I or he or she can't find or doesn't want to find Christ in the midst of this situation or relationship. It's time to go back to the story of the disciples who ignored almost to the point of drowning, the presence of Christ in the boat.

Fear is not born of storms, but of self-centered lives. Terror can haunt our innards even on a glassy sea. Storm is the gift that names our helplessness and drives us beyond ourselves to the Other. Squalls happen for the sake of faith.

They Said to One Another

"Who can this be that the wind and the sea obey him?" is not a question that can be answered once and for all. We talk about God so easily. I suspect that is because of our idolatrous belief in God as *concept*, a notion to be analyzed, categorized, and intellectually possessed. The Israelites knew better. They experienced God. They took their shoes off in God's presence, hid their faces, and marveled that they lived through it. They never pronounced God's name because they never presumed the gift of a first-name familiarity with the Lord God. An authentic experience of God was and is marked by reverential awe and a recognition of mystery: a question that has multiple correct responses but is never answered. Those who are so definitive about their God, whose relationship with Jesus is always comfortable, have settled for a lesser God.

Catechists are prone to once-and-for-all answers. The Lord God evokes wonder.

Summing Up

Looking back at this Gospel narrative, we see all the elements of a good catechumenate. Let *us* cross over: mutual journey, ongoing conversion. Leaving the crowd: following Christ is counter-cultural; the farther shore is the face of death. They climbed into the same boat with Jesus: *the whole purpose of the trip is to understand what that means.* Squalls clarify the issue. Only Christ can order the storm. Desist, be still and see: I am God. Why are you terrified? Faith recognizes Christ's presence; fear keeps bailing water. They kept asking; there is no once-and-for-all answer.

A lecture on faith could hardly have been as effective as allowing the disciples to discover his presence and power in a terrifying squall. Understanding follows experience. So should the lecture. That's Methodology 101 for the catechumenal journey. The catechist draws out the journeyers' own death/life experiences, allows time to find the sleeping Christ in those moments, then asks the faith question "What are your terrors— why cling to them?" This in turn surfaces the deeper question "Who can this Christ be?"—a question of unlimited possibility. There is no final answer. The question seduces us on into deeper and deeper understanding. They *kept on asking* one another.

For Discussion

- Read paragraph 1 of the *Rite of Christian Initiation of Adults*; Mark Searle's article "Journey of Conversion," *Worship* (1980): 35-55; and James Dunning's article "Conversion: Being Born Again and Again and Again," *Catholic Update* (April 1988). Conversion is at the heart of the catechumenal process. Discuss as a team what you understand to be the steps of conversion. In your own faith journey, name one or two conversion times. Reflect on one such time. Who was involved? What precipitated the conversion? What was the change? How do you know the change has happened? How is it confirmed? What is the role of faith, of the community, of prayer?

- To be authentic in this ministry, each person needs to be aware of the moments of conversion in his or her own life. Most of these moments deepen our faith; few of us have dramatic moments, though that is always a possibility.

- What do you understand to be the role of the team in this period? In what ways do you help others on their conversion journey?

- As a team, is there concern regarding numbers of people in the process? Are you willing to do this process for one? Conversion is not a "feel good" mentality but rather a process of embracing the cross of Jesus Christ.

- Based on this section, how does the team understand the "elements of a good catechumenate"?

The Rite Application

In the rite, the introduction to the catechumenal period begins thus: "Leave your country and come into the land I will show you." Here it is again, this business of crossing over. No doubt, it is a rite of passage.

Passage is something most Catholics understand little of. That is because Catholics of the last thousand years have been primarily *conservationists*, keepers of the faith, clerics whose duty is to maintain the archives of truth. We have proudly stood our ground as a bastion of solidarity in the midst of a world shaken by the continuing reformation of its shifting layers of living sub-strata. But along came Vatican II, a veritable earthquake, cracking the Roman rock to expose its component pebbles: the people of God. Behold! The Roman citadel rests on living rock! A fact never denied but empirically ignored for centuries. We are as yet uncomfortable with it. Living rock moves. That means changing, reshaping, leveling mountains, and filling valleys. It means making way for the Lord.

The switch from conservation to transformation is difficult. It is, in fact, diametrically opposed. There is an angry insistence by many, intentional clerics of whatever style collar, that the catechumenate is soft on doctrine. They are deluding themselves; the anger is a mask. The real issue cannot be about doctrine; the Rite of Christian Initiation of Adults is superbly grounded in Scripture and tradition, the twin fonts of revelation, out of which all doctrine flows. The masked issue is the loss of comfortable conservationism. To conserve, one only has to be intractable, protective and "right." To transform, one must assume the risk of the unfinished. Vatican II, in the document *Lumen Gentium* (*Dogmatic Constitution on the Church*), plainly states that we are in fact a "pilgrim Church [which] in its sacraments and institutions...carries the mark of this world which will pass, and she herself takes her place among the creatures who groan and travail yet and await the revelation of the sons of God" (48). Like it or not we bear the mark of the unfinished.

It is important to name this ancient fear of being an imperfect church and courageously buy into the mentality of pilgrimage or passage. We certainly cannot understand or properly implement the rite while clinging to conservationism.

The Manner of Passage

According to the *Rite of Christian Initiation of Adults*, the transformative process, or Christian passage, is brought about by an experience of the sacred, the divine presence through the Word, ordinary Christian life, liturgical rites and apostolic works. Building upon the first faith, conversion, repentance, prayer, and sense of church nurtured in the precatechumenate, the rite names four ways in which this passage to maturity is brought about (75):

> 1. Provide a suitable catechesis, accommodated to the liturgical year and solidly supported by celebrations of the Word, which offers the catechumens not only an acquaintance with dogma, but a "profound sense of the mystery of salvation."

2. By the example of sponsors, godparents, and the entire Christian community, the candidates will become familiar with the Christian way of life; that is they will learn ready prayer, faith witness, Christian hope, obedience to the Spirit, and love of neighbor even at the cost of oneself. This spiritual journey, which brings about a progressive change of outlook and conduct, is made manifest in social consequences.

3. The church helps them along the way, purifying and strengthening them, as a mother would, with appropriate rituals.

4. The candidates apprentice in the mission of the church by the witness of their lives and by actively spreading the Good News.

In a single paragraph, the rite has captured the essence of conversion catechesis. For those looking for a "curriculum" here it is in a nutshell. But for the "rite application," the nut needs to be cracked open.

Suitable Catechesis

According to the rite, the catechumenate is a period of formation in *Christian living*. Consequently, "suitable catechesis" is concerned primarily with a profound sense of the mystery of salvation, the mystery of life in Christ; secondarily it offers an "acquaintance with dogmas and precepts." All of this is "solidly supported by celebrations of the word" accommodated to the liturgical year (RCIA 75). There are several important and separate issues here.

First of all, by separating the issues of dogma and salvation, the church officially recognizes that knowledge and Christian living are not necessarily coterminous realities. She also makes it very clear which is of the essence; it is "training in Christian life" (RCIA 75). Those who have ears to hear, let them hear! A catechumenate that is essentially instructional without grounding in the experience of Christian living, is abortive. It does not support life. Rather, a major part of the catechesis must be insertion into the common life of the Christian community, not just the Sunday assembly. As Aidan Kavanagh insists, "one learns how to fast, pray, repent, celebrate and serve the good of one's neighbor less by being lectured on these matters than by close association with people who do these things with regular ease and flair" ("Christian Initiation of Adults: The Rites" 122). Mission begins now, not in mystagogia.

Secondly, the rite does require an appropriate acquaintance with dogmas which is *solidly supported by celebrations of the Word accommodated to the liturgical year.* In other words, the doctrine of the church is not flotsam dredged from outer space but affirmations arising out of Scripture and tradition and articulated through the experience of the faithful. As such, doctrine should be explored as it naturally arises out of the lectionary and the liturgical year. Even as I write these words, I can hear the roar of objections: you won't come across all the basic doctrine that way, it takes too long, everything can't be covered, what about the sacraments, etc. Right. There *isn't* enough time; you can't shove all the important stuff in a nine-month "program." That's why the *National Statutes for the Catechumenate* requires a minimum of one year from acceptance into the order of catechumens through initiation/acceptance into the church (6). That's why the rite itself states that the catechumenate is an extended period of time—"several years if necessary"—and that nothing regarding the duration of this period can be determined *a priori* (RCIA 76). The rationale behind the minimum of one full year is that the catechumens will at least be exposed to the substance of one entire Gospel in that cycle and that, within the course of a complete Gospel and within the celebration of one liturgical year, most of our basic tenets of faith will be encountered. That is the beginning of an "appropriate acquaintance" with church dogma.

It is important not to pass so quickly over paragraph 75.1 as to miss the directive that catechesis is based on the *celebration* of the Word within the liturgical year. It not only means that we use the lectionary for our text, but that catechesis is rooted in liturgy. This automatically includes as solid support for dogma not only Scripture but also tradition, both of which are ritually incarnated within the worship cycle of the church. The theological norm *Lex orandi, lex credendi* upholds the essential bond between faith and prayer. Literally, this Latin axiom means that the law of praying is the law of believing. In other words the central affirmations of the church's liturgy are the norms of our belief. That idea is certainly not new with Vatican II. It has been axiomatic throughout most of church history, probably originating in the mid-fifth century with Prosper of Aquitane, a disciple of Augustine (McBrien 541). It has been a guiding norm upheld through Trent and Vatican I and to the present day. Centuries of minimalistic liturgy in a language we did not understand made it difficult at times for the faithful to know what prayer/belief was being celebrated. But now that the full birthright of the church's prayer is in the process of restoration, we have the opportunity and need to rediscover the rich theology of our worship. Religious educators and liturgists must come to common vision. Separatists within these ministries can no longer be tolerated. The faith/prayer experience is a seamless garment and the fabric of Christian catechesis.

Christian Living

The jig is up. All the jockeying for curricula and pet projects in the catechumenate, the fantastic manipulations, argumentations and hallucinations of the parish pundits are undone. In these five sentences the rite ends all our machinations about the making of Christians:

> As they become familiar with the Christian way of life and are helped by the example and support of sponsors, godparents, and the entire Christian community, the catechumens learn to turn more readily to God in prayer, to bear witness to the faith, in all things to keep their hopes set on Christ, to follow supernatural inspiration in their deeds, and to practice love of neighbor, even at the cost of self-renunciation. Thus formed, the newly converted set out on a spiritual journey. Already sharing through faith in the mystery of Christ's death and resurrection, they pass from the old to a new nature made perfect in Christ. Since this transition brings with it a progressive change of outlook and conduct, it should become manifest by means of its social consequences and it should develop gradually during the period of the catechumenate. Since the Lord in whom they believe is a sign of contradiction, the newly converted often experience divisions and separations, but they also taste the joy that God gives without measure (RCIA 75.2).

If you can't believe Aidan Kavanagh, believe the rite. It says that catechesis begins with example. A Christ-discipling community is the first ingredient in conversion catechesis. If the parish community is essentially self-nurturing, self-righteous and self-saving, the jig is indeed up. How can one learn to be Christian in a self-proselytizing system? That is not to say that parishes which draw large numbers of catechumens are necessarily living a robust Christian life. The B.P.O.E. and the Elvis Presley Fan Club draw large numbers, but a fraternity of people with similar tastes does not define Christian community. By their fruits, you will know. The rite names the fruits. They are ready prayer, faithful witness, Christ-centered hope,

Spirit-informed acts, and the lifestyle (practice) of self-renouncing love of neighbor.

This description of the fruit of Christian life is reminiscent of the entire fifth chapter in Matthew's Gospel which calls for a whole new way of living. Beginning with the Beatitudes, this new way of being is developed through a series of reversed attitudes ("You have heard....But I say...") culminating with the famous "Be perfect, therefore, as your heavenly Father is perfect" (Mt 5:48). This is a summary of what was said before it; as such, its meaning rests more critically than ever on its context. The word "perfect" may be a legitimate translation of the Greek, but the common connotation of it today is far too reflective of individual self-polishing to properly convey this context. The original Greek word literally means "whole, integral, undivided" (*Theological Dictionary* vol. 8, 75). It refers to the new attitude that Jesus has just demanded of his disciples, a wholeness of heart that means going far beyond the letter of the law, loving those who persecute and harm you as well as your friends. It delineates an inclusive rather than exclusive bias in which holiness becomes a communal affair. Such is the undividedness, the wholeness of the love of your heavenly Father, who gives sun and rain to the just and the unjust without prejudice (*Good News According to Matthew* 131-5). The perfection called for is not self-polishing; it is full, unlimited love which leaves no one out. The rite assumes this to be the journey of the ordinary Christian way of life.

For the first time in a millennium, the Catholic church officially holds up this "perfection" as normative for ordinary Christian life. In the Dogmatic Constitution on the Church, there is this historic one-liner: "All the faithful, whatever their condition or state...are called by the Lord to that perfection of sanctity by which the Father himself is perfect." This is followed by a full chapter on the call to holiness to which "all the faithful are invited and obliged [according to] their own state of life" (*Lumen Gentium* 11.3 and 42.5) The rite reiterates the call by assuming that catechumens can learn heroic Christian virtues by being in the midst of the lives of ordinary Christians. This is a life jolt for Catholics who have been told explicitly and implicitly since the fifth century that only priests and religious were in that elite group of perfection-seekers. Without a doubt, this restored apostolic attitude about the holiness of ordinary Christian life is both exciting and terrifying.

I believe that the white-knuckled clinging (overtly or covertly) to the convert-instruction model of the past is rooted in a number of hidden fears, not the least of which is the fear of embracing our own holiness. Maybe this is the unnamed terror that lurks in our hearts as we attempt to implement the catechumenate. Could it be that the Hound of Heaven has finally caught up with us? If we commit to the Rite of Christian Initiation of Adults in all its implications, it will surely be a day of reckoning, a day of suicide or prophecy, as Ralph suggests. We Christians, of "whatever condition or state," will have to look holiness full in the face. For me, a lay person, this evokes both satisfaction (it's about time we were acknowledged!) and the fearful recognition that when it comes to sanctity I can no longer use the clergy and religious as my scapegoats for holiness. For clergy and religious no less, it may well be a long and discomforting look. Have our religious and ecclesial structures encouraged the production of moral activists instead of prophets and confessors?

It is my bias that this considerable excursus into the holiness of Christian life is not only justified but imperative in any discussion of initiation. I think this is a significant area which is frequently overlooked in our approach to initiation. Holiness of the basic Christian community is a fact, and therefore an assumption of the rite, an assumption echoed by theologians like Aidan Kavanagh, who speaks of Christians who celebrate and serve with "regular ease and flair." Unfortunately, the laity generally assumes no such thing. As we have already indicated, there are historical reasons for this. Since the time of Augustine, the church has cultivated a caste system of holiness. At the bottom of Christian endeavor was the "way of the commandments" relegated to ordinary people like moms and dads and business folks. Then there was a quantum leap to the holiest of endeavors, the "way of perfection" walked by the virgins and celibates of this world, those with priestly orders or religious vows. Now that the church has publicly disavowed this stance and returned holiness to the public domain, we have to take a new look at what it means to be holy.

It is no surprise that our understanding of the way to holiness has largely been transmuted through this perverse evolution into a ladder of self-improvement. We have inherited a moralistic piety which is pitifully pelagian. Believing that we climb the ladder to holiness by performing moral acts, we attempt our own salvation by trying to become moral decathletes. Wrong. Wrong for us, wrong for our catechumens. We are already holy people, and it is not we who made ourselves so. It is God who has made us God's own dear children; holiness is our unearned inheritance. Our challenge is not to squander or cheapen it but to learn how to live a life-style in harmony with this royal heritage, to live graciously. What saves the catechumenate, conversion, and Christianity from an elitist endeavor is this: it is not moral acts that make us holy; rather it is holiness with which we are lavishly gifted that issues forth in moral living (Untener).

It is important for us to understand this distinction between morality and holiness. The roots of the words themselves bring great clarity to the issue. Holy derives from the Greek root, *holos*, that which makes whole. Morality comes to us from the Latin *moris*, indicating custom or manners. The first defines being, the later describes behavior. Who you are, who you see yourself to be determines your behavior, not the other way around. Learning moral theology will never make saints. Holiness is not taught or learned; it is a gift. We can only learn how to honor the gift, to give thanks, and to model its gracious use for others. This facet of conversion is learning how to quit bailing water, how to turn around and accept the gift of life already there in Christ Jesus. The resultant relationship is what brings about "progressive change of outlook and conduct" which in turn manifests itself in social consequences.

Finally, this whole issue of Christian living is a modifier of the previous section on "suitable catechesis." Lectionary-based catechesis can become as deadly as any other form of instruction if it is not rooted in living. I think that catechumenate teams look (sometimes feverishly) for subject matter outside the lectionary because their Scripture-sharing is not substantive. Failure to apply the Gospel to life and attitudinal issues reduces the content to a safe intellectual arena which becomes dry, repetitious, unchallenging and non-converting. Ralph says that boredom is "the experience of having to attend constantly to the insignificant" (142). "Insignificant" is a term that can too often be applied to the catechist's questions about the Sunday Scriptures, questions frequently theoretical and significant of nothing in the world of dying and rising. But no one is bored when the Gospel challenge is clearly a death threat to personal attitudes and lifestyles. No one accepts this gauntlet with a yawn. The difference between talking about Scripture and breaking open the Word is throwing down the gauntlet: what does this mean in *my* life and what will it *cost me* to take it seriously?

Ritual: Mother Knows Best

"The Church, like a mother, helps the catechumens on their journey by means of suitable liturgical rites...." Mothers understand ritual. They probably invented it. Mothers instinctively know that children learn identity and purpose through rituals: hand-washing and prayer before meals, sharing food and sharing toys, the bedtime story and the tucking-in, the sending off to school, the kissing and the unctioning of a scrape, the holiday traditions, the grounding for rules transgressed, and the rites of passage. So too, Mother Church forms and roots her newest ones in the family traditions and strengthens them with unctions and blessings.

The catechumenate, beginning with the Rite of Acceptance into the Catechumenate, is rooted all along the way in liturgical celebrations of the Word, and is sustained throughout by minor exorcisms, blessings and anointings. It ends with the ritual of the chosen, the "Election." We are told in a Vatican II document that "love never expressed dies" (*Music in Catholic Worship* 4). These rites are the love ministrations of a mother who knows how to bring forth and nurture life. Those who are irritated by these "nuisance rites that clutter up the Mass" or who relegate the rites to "nice little add-ons to the instruction" are fundamentally unready for initiation ministry, unattuned as they are to the rituals of life and love. They are probably also out of touch with other affective activities such as music and art appreciation, poetry and love-making and sacramental celebrations in general.

But the nature of ritual is more than just a celebration of love. The wordy activity that goes on from week to week throughout the catechumenal process can trap and lose us in problem-solving meanderings. Rite cuts through all that and drops us cleanly into the transcendent, paradoxically articulating through symbolic activity inexpressible mystery. Ritual is our door to the sacred. In this integrating encounter with the sacred, our scattered life forces are brought to focus and we receive the conviction and strength to press on. Rite calls up the memory of who we are and what we are about in a way no mere words can communicate or direct. It is important that catechists and teams make good use of the minor rites offered during the catechumenate, for, as the rite says, it is by these that the catechumens are purified and strengthened. As a church we are, perhaps, too invested in male values: getting the job done, being right, ordering, and legalizing (categories of achievement and authority). There is nothing wrong with these values; they are simply incomplete. The active must be balanced by the receptive, progress must be rooted in memory, and articulation must be completed by symbolism. These latter feminine values are incarnated in the rituals and rich symbols of the church. God does not need liturgy—the rituals of worship—but people do (*Environment and Art in Catholic Worship* 4). Ritual is a way faith gets out of our heads and into the whole of us. Mother really does know best.

Apostolic Mission

The rite names one final means of formation and guidance during the catechumenate: that the catechumens be actively engaged in mission. It says this very clearly: "catechumens should also learn how to work actively with others to spread the Gospel and build up the church by the witness of their lives...." It is amazing to me that there is nevertheless a wide-spread misconception that mission is supposed to be "saved" until mystagogia. The only logical explanation I can imagine for this mentality is that catechumenate teams don't know what else to do after Easter and that if they do the "mission thing" during the catechumenate, then they can't "use" it again in mystagogia. It may be consoling to note that mission is a life-long project, and there will probably be enough "to go around" through both the catechumenate and mystagogia. Moreover, the initiation process is not a bag of tricks to be performed in proper succession, but a ritual of the divine-human encounter, the experiences of which are continually cycling and deepening. Mission is not a project, it does not translate into busy work for the Lord; rather it is faith spilling over into living. The bottom-line reality is that without mission the conversion enterprise is a hoax.

More specifically, what is mission? We get mission, minister and ministry all jumbled together in a kind of religious stew. Mission is generic to a life of Christian discipleship. "As the Father has sent me, I also send you." *Ite, missa est.* Go, you are sent—teach them whatever I have told you, love as I have loved, make disciples of all nations. Go, go—you are missioned. Christian discipleship means that you are co-missioned with Christ to bring into reality the kingdom of God.

Minister and ministry are not generic but very specific. A minister is an agent designated to act in a specific capacity in subservience to the will of another. Any appointed or elected official is a minister of his or her political body. The "order" of holy orders is the designation to presbyteral ministry within the polity of the church. Other liturgical roles such as lector, cantor, or extraordinary minister of the Eucharist, though not to be conflated with sacramental orders, are ministries as well. These individuals are designees for specific capacities or functions for the good of the whole. To call *everything* we do as Christians "ministry" is to disorder the Body of Christ. The *mission* of the Body of Christ is to bring life, abundantly, to all. *Ministry* is the functional ordering of the Body role by role. Mission can, but not necessarily, be expressed in designated ministry.

The rite does not speak of finding ministerial slots for the candidates, but counsels them to learn how to be missionaries: to spread the Good News and to build up the Body of Christ by the witness of their living. That is not primarily or even ideally expressed through specific jobs in the church community such as being on committees for church clean-up, hospitality, the church bazaar, community outreach or even prayer groups. It does mean that discipling Christ should be making a difference in their living, whatever they do. It means that their actions speak the nearness of the kingdom, and as of old, others will know they are Christians by their love.

What does all this require of the catechumenate team? Certainly it means that our lives should be examples of true mission. Additionally, we need to provide ways to help the candidates and catechumens discern whether or not their lives are changing, and if so, in what direction. If one's journey is an enterprise in self-polishing it will issue in self-righteousness or bitter depression. Its fruit will be isolation rather than incorporation. On the other hand, a journey truly centered on Christ bears fruit in relationship, issuing in a robust but unpretentious interest in the health of the whole body of Christ and an awareness of the value of its most inelegant member. But there are many subtle variations of these themes, and people play them out with fits and starts, making it difficult to identify real direction; our own clouded perceptions and misdirections muck things up even more. It is essential therefore that sufficient opportunities for, and authentic instruments of discernment be made available to the catechumens and candidates. This may be difficult to do, since by and large the gift of spiritual direction is not freely exercised today outside of religious communities. The general lack of this ministry may be a factor in the purportedly significant drop-out rate of neophytes nation-wide. Over the long haul the fabric of the new Christian life may fall apart because Christian witness did not become the warp and woof of daily living—and such gross misdirection was never discerned!

The whole area of spiritual direction, ancient as it is in our Catholic tradition, became an art lost to the average lay person, relegated as it was for so many centuries to cloisters and confessionals, and finally pragmaticized right out of confessionals as well. (Valid form and matter was all that counted.) It is ironic. Private, frequent confession which developed in the monastic era did not arise out of a need for radical reconciliation, but for spiritual direction. Confession began as the confidences of soul friend to soul friend in the pursuit of holiness! Today the catechumenate process is fertile ground for the eventual re-birth of the soul-friend concept within the framework and needs of our times. According to the rite, sponsors are to stand witness to their candidate's "moral character, faith and intention" (RCIA 10). To witness to these things implies a rather deep level of spiritual intercommunication, descriptive of a soul friend relationship. The rite further describes the godparents as those who personally practice Gospel living, and are therefore able to sustain the candidates in moments of anxiety and to guide their progress in the baptismal life (RCIA 11). Quite clearly, these are elements of spiritual direction. In this instance the church reiterates again that responsibility for holiness comes to rest on all Christians, both lay and ordered. Such responsibility can only be met in Christ, and through much prayer and fasting. Spiritual discernment guides us in true discipling which is the heart and marrow of Christian mission: the establishment of the kingdom in the life of the world.

What are some of the tools that can help in the process of discernment? In addition to spiritual direction—journaling, interviewing, sponsor-candidate trust, team communication with the sponsors, ongoing opportunities for prayer and meditative time—are all important opportunities for clarification, for coming to grips with the tell-tale signs of faithed or faithless living. The way we help catechumens learn how to build up the church by the witness of their lives is by prayer, example and discernment, not by giving them busy work.

Apostolic mission is neither self-serving activism nor a "groupyism" that demands we buy into a bandwagon pietistic fantasy. Rather it is the challenge of being sent as Christ was sent. That has never been easy. When the hosannas of Passion Sunday died down in the silence of the cross, there stood by Jesus in his dying one lone disciple, his mother, and a couple of other women.

For Discussion

- Read *Sharing the Light of Faith* (Washington, DC: USCC, 1978), paying close attention to chapter 5 and paragraphs 170-178.

- Word, worship, community, service are the four components of pastoral formation as named in the *General Catechetical Directory,* in RCIA 75, and in centuries of church tradition. In your process, determine the amount of time and energy given to each component in the catechumenate period. Why is this? The emphasis in the ritual text is that of "training in Christian life." How is your process doing or not doing this?

- One of the tensions of this period is the question of information. The catechumens/candidates need to know the teachings of the church. What do you consider to be the key teachings? Place this list alongside chapter 5 of *Sharing the Light of Faith.*

- In the *Introduction to the Roman Missal,* Pope Paul VI states that Scripture is to be the foundation of all theological study. The ritual text places emphasis on celebrations of the Word and dismissal of the catechumens following the homily. This invites reflection and discussion on the Sunday readings as well as the teaching of the church that flows from the celebration. On a scale of one to ten, how are you doing? Explain.

- The rite also provides blessings, minor exorcisms, and anointings. In what ways are you using these at every gathering?

- Discuss ways in which apostolic mission is incorporated into the process at this time. Note the particular the line, "Mission is not a project, it does not translate into busy work for the Lord; rather it is faith spilling over into living." What is your understanding of "mission"?

The Rite Mentality

All good ritual is rooted in memory, pregnant memory that brings forth new life to the present. This is especially so in liturgical celebrations of the Word in which the family story and tradition are renewed and incarnated in those who have ears to truly hear. We are told in the *Lectionary for Mass: Introduction* that liturgy and the Word are fundamentally interlocked.

> The more profound our understanding of the liturgical
> celebration, the higher our appreciation of the
> importance of God's word. Whatever we say of the one,
> we can in turn say of the other, because each recalls the
> mystery of Christ and each in its own way *causes that*
> *mystery to be ever present* (5, my emphasis).

The document goes on to say that the Word of God is held in equal reverence with the eucharistic mystery, naming Word and Eucharist as twin sources of the church's sustenance. "The Church is nourished spiritually at the table of the God's Word and at the table of the Eucharist: from the one it grows in wisdom and from the other in holiness" (10). The rite mentality of the catechumenal period is this: the liturgical celebration of the Word is its backbone, and this liturgical celebration does not end with dismissal. The breaking open of that Word outside of Mass should be done with flair and a continuing sense of ritual, rooted in the dangerous memories of a people covenanted with a God inexorably committed to death for resurrection. The dismissal of the catechumens is itself a ritual of memory, a remembering that all of life in Christ is pure gift, and that every one of us await with thanks the eventual gifting of ultimate union.

Endings and Beginnings

Major human rituals have their singular times and seasons, marking as they do, epic events. They are celebrations of both endings and beginnings, of continuity and discontinuity. Marriage, for example, celebrates but does not create a union of love between two people. Such love has been growing for some time. Thus marriage does not ritualize the beginning of union, but ritualizes the state of it. The marriage ritual is in this way an instrument of continuity and commitment. At the same time, marriage celebrates discontinuity, the ending of the old and the beginning of the new way of life. The moment of this ending and beginning may be arbitrary, but the covenant it announces is not. It bespeaks real death and rebirth into new life. Major ritual situates us in the manner of our living.

But human life is full of lesser rites that consecrate the every day struggles. Moments of wine and friendship, of bound wounds and shared shoulders, of competition and team enterprise, of picnics and barbershop quartets—these are rituals that transcend the tick-tock measuring of life and bring to each metered moment, value and orientation in relationship. It is by reason of these lesser rites that we find encouragement to keep covenant.

In this same way, the church marks and celebrates with public rites the major stages in Christian initiation: acceptance,

election and the initiatory sacraments, marking thereby significant moments of continuity and commitment, and of death
and rebirth. But she also consecrates the more ordinary
moments and daily struggles with blessings, exorcisms and
anointings. Like those lesser human rites, these rites are
celebrated when, in sensitivity, the moment calls for it. Thus,
blessings are given, as in human ritual, as signs of love and
tender care, bestowed as encouragement and affirmation along
the way of life. Exorcisms are moments of staunch defense
against evil, a strengthening and reorientation in times of
difficulty. Anointing is a yet more powerful touch of healing
and strength for those in a painful place as well as a fragrant
reminder of the catechumens' shared life in the Anointed One.

The Rites of the Chosen

That sounds terribly elitist. It tends to grind against the
American perception of equal rights. Yet in a democratic
society election should be a comfortable concept. The rites of
the chosen have always orchestrated the seasons of political life.
All may have the right to run for office, but few, very few are
chosen. And the right to pass on authority with respect to
human life is in the hands of those to whom God has
entrusted it: the people. So too with the church. Many are
called, but few are chosen. The privilege of choice which
belongs to Christ has in this case also been delegated. It resides
in the members of his Body. It is the awesome duty and
privilege of the people of the community to give valid witness
in behalf of those seeking election. And it is the obligation of
the bishop or his delegate to respond in fidelity to that witness.
That is what the Rite of Election is all about.

Election takes place for the sake of the common good, the
health of the whole body, and for clear definition of what it
means to be Christian. The responsibility of the discerning

process for election rests conjunctively with the pastor, the catechumenal team, and the sponsor or godparent of each individual. This is a responsibility that cannot be ignored. Neither can it be approached from a largely proselytic attitude. In the past, it seemed that the only thing of importance was that the waters of baptism were poured. In spite of a protracted preparation period, it seems the mentality has not changed greatly. Few catechumenates really go through a discernment process. In most cases, any warm body is not only elected but incorporated. But lack of courage on the part of the pastoral team to discern unreadiness as well as readiness depreciates the Christian commitment, encourages shallow motivation, dilutes and/or disrupts the ongoing journey, and ultimately runs the risk of upending conversion and reducing it to a membership drive. By the same token, folding to the demands of a time-line demonstrates that expediency exercises priority over establishing the kingdom.

The task of discernment should be ongoing throughout the process, a joint venture in mutual prayer and careful listening in which the pastor and his team discern *with* the candidate whether the time is ripe for this individual to commit to final preparation for full incorporation into the baptismal and eucharistic life of the church.

The backbone of the rite itself is the community's witness to the bishop on behalf of those to be elected. Since the community has delegated its electoral discernment to the pastor and the catechumenate team as those who best know these individuals, it should be noted that in a very real sense, the absence of appropriate discernment on the part of the pastoral team opens the community to misinformed witnessing and reduces the election and enrollment of names to ritualized pabulum. No one will perceive this more clearly than the Elect themselves who, as they sign their names in the Book of the Elect, are deprived of the deep sense of fidelity and commitment honed in the process of discernment. The meeting with the bishop in the company of the legions called in faith throughout the broader church will always give one a profound sense of unity and catholicity; but whether or not it offers a sense of apostleship and holiness depends in large measure on the authenticity of the call to conversion.

If valid witnessing is the backbone of this rite, the bishop is the heart of it. Given the size and structure of today's church, the initiation process may be not only the richest time but perhaps the only time the bishop can really exercise his role as Family Elder. It is an almost unique and certainly rare opportunity to be father to a fruitful flock. Warmth, genuine joy and paternal accessibility on the part of the bishop can make the difference between good ritual that calls forth rootedness and fidelity and poor ritual that isolates and destroys the deeper sensitivities. As a father, the bishop should also strengthen the Elect for the intense preparation time ahead of purification and enlightenment by making his presence and his blessing symbol and pledge of the prayerful support and unity of the entire Body of Christ.

For Discussion

- Read paragraph 76 in the *Rite of Christian Initiation of Adults.* Since "nothing, therefore, can be settled a priori," what is the length of the catechumenate? Discernment for the Rite of Election is of utmost importance. Discernment is carried on throughout the process, not just prior to a major rite. It is done in the context of mutual prayer, with the catechumen/candidate, with the sponsor under the guidance of the Holy Spirit.

- What is the criteria for election? It is found in paragraph 78 as well as in the dialogue of paragraph

131, options A and B. The team cannot judge the heart of another person but, as paragraph 43 states, "outward indication of such dispositions."

- As a parish, it is important to know the diocesan practice for such questions as: Who signs the Book of the Elect? When is it signed? Where and when is the Rite of Election? The team must also know that if a marriage case has not been resolved, the catechumen/candidate must wait because the Rite of Election calls them to the sacraments at "the next Easter Vigil." This reality is what prompts—demands— that a parish provide an on-going catechumenate so that those who discern that this is *not* the right time or who are unable to celebrate the rite of election can continue in the pastoral formation. They do not "start over" or go into a "holding pattern" until the case is resolved; rather, they continue to participate in the community's life and prayer and pastoral formation.

- In light of this section, in what ways have you been affirmed and/or challenged? What needs to continue in your process? Why? What needs to change? Why? How will this change take place?

Part Three

Purification and Enlightenment

"Close encounters through the looking glass"

FOCAL ISSUES: sin and salvation

What Are Purification
and Enlightenment?

Jesus went out again beside the sea....He saw Levi son of
Alphaeus sitting at the tax booth, and he said to him,
"Follow me." And he got up and followed him.

And as he sat at dinner in Levi's house, many tax
collectors and sinners were also sitting with Jesus and his
disciples....When the scribes of the Pharisees saw that he
was eating with sinners and tax collectors, they said to
his disciples, "Why does he eat with tax collectors and
sinners?" When Jesus heard this, he said to them, "Those
who are well have no need of a physician, but those who
are sick; I have come to call not the righteous but
sinners" (Mk 2:13-17).

I remember vividly a particular planning session of a liturgy
preparation team with whom I used to work. The Gospel
for that Sunday was Matthew 9:9-13, the parallel passage of
the Marcan text quoted above. It seemed to me the issue was,
at least in part, sinners and the self-righteous. From the drift

of the Gospel story, it was also my bias that "sinner" was clearly the preferential position, and that we ought to celebrate the fact that all of us fall without exception into that category! Much to my astonishment, no one else shared my delight. The rest of the group was caught up in dark rejection of the very word sinner. They thought that a universal statement of sinship would be offensive to the folks in the assembly. Well, I guess "sinner" can be an ugly word, a besmirchment of an individual's character, a classifying of the worst sort, a disfiguring of the upstance we love to model within the community. It would certainly be all of this if we thought for a moment that we could, on our own account, be called good. But I remember that Jesus rejected the attribute even for himself, applying goodness to God alone (Mk 10:18). The truth is that either we recognize our sinfulness or succumb to the idolatry of self-righteousness.

Sinfulness is a badly misunderstood state of affairs, dumped by bemused believers into the same bucket with "sins." Some spend an entire lifetime confessing, controlling, and avoiding *sins* without ever identifying *sin* in their lives. This is the basic *non sequitur* in the mentality of the self-righteous. The difference between sins and sin can be seen most easily in the story of the prodigal son. The younger son was full of sins, but the older son was full of sin. Sin closes out the love of the Father and intimate union. Bitterness, resentment, and personal alienation are trademarks of sinfulness and are countersigns of the kingdom. No matter how good a Christian I think I am, if I am bitter because I am taken for granted or because my talents go unappreciated, if I am resentful because my children don't live up to my expectations, if I am bitter about clericalism or the hierarchical church, "if I am bitter about anything...I am brimming over with sin, even if I don't have many sins" (Westley 166 for this quotation as well as for the general comparison of sin and sinfulness). Recognizing sinfulness names my alienation and opens the possibility of finding reunion and the sweetness of love. Sin is division and alienation; the opposite of sin is grace—the gift of intimate union. To admit that I am a sinner is not to say that I am bad but that I am loved and that at this time and in certain ways I have not loved well in return. To know this allows me to make better choices and, like the prodigal, to seek open doors. Understanding that I am sinful is the beginning of Good News.

The flip side of being sinful is being saved. The word "salvation" is one that eluded my understanding for years. There's much talk about being saved, much of which is individualistic, evasive and childish. For some, salvation simply means getting through the pearly gates. This concept effectively sweeps the salvation issue neatly out of the present and into the untouchable afterlife—and conveniently out of my hands. The salvation question becomes unanswerable in this lifetime. Others think salvation is had simply by *saying* that you have it: by "claiming" Jesus as my personal savior. This reminds me of my three-year-old grandson's gleeful declaration at the end of *every* game: "I winned, you losed!" regardless of the prevailing evidence. Having salvation merely by claiming it is not only childish, but also neatly evasive. Once I stake my claim, it is once again, out of my hands.

In view of such half-baked understandings, the question of salvation can only produce consummate confusion. The confusion comes from mechanizing salvation, as if it were something external that is done *to* us. Clarity came for me with the realization that salvation is like faith, it is a way of leaning into life. Salvation happens each time we open ourselves to life already redeemed in Christ instead of clinging to destruction and death. It is consummation, bringing life to completion moment by moment. Salvation is had by each and every choice to live gracefully and intimately in and with the holy One; a choice made possible in the power of his redeeming self-gift.

Sin and salvation are the polarizing issues, the magnetic energy that drew the Son of God into the field of human death and life. They are the darkness and light in every human life. Wrestling with sin and salvation is what the rite calls purification and enlightenment. Sooner or later, anyone discipling with Christ must reckon with these forces. Lent is the acceptable time.

For Discussion

- How do you as a team define purification? enlightenment? In the same manner, how do you define sin? grace? How has your understanding of sin and grace changed and/or deepened and/or expanded over the years? What prompted this growth in understanding?

- In what ways does sin impact your lives? What are the many dimensions of sin? In what ways does grace impact your lives?

- How do you define "salvation"? How does this dialogue remind you of your discussion of conversion? Is there a connection between conversion and sin and grace? How do you understand the connection?

The Jesus Approach

The story of Jesus and Levi cannot be used as a line-by-line methodology for the period of purification and enlightenment. Rather this story is a reminder about the heart of the matter which, according the very words of the rite, is "a deeper knowledge of Christ the Savior." Knowledge of Christ the Savior is profoundly different from acknowledging Christ as the Savior. The first is a function of intimacy that invites transformation; the second is a simple assessment of the situation, more deeply related to order than to relationship. There is nothing wrong with that, but it bypasses the internal dynamic of conversion. In this business of becoming Catholic or joining any religion for that matter, we tend to get all involved with ecclesiastical formulas as if salvation depended on doing the church thing right. So when it comes time for purification, for scrutinizing ourselves before the Lord, we often mistake the law for the Lord, using it instead of him for the measure of our righteousness. It was the Pharisees' mistake, too. They who did everything right, who had so few sins, would have nothing to do with these "offenders of the law" whose lives were full of sins.

But in the story of Levi, Jesus challenges all those presumptions. As the story unfolds, we notice that Jesus saw Levi for what he was, a tax collector, a man of sins. "Follow me," Christ said. Levi "got up" (like the prodigal) and followed him. Jesus responded with intimacy; he shared a meal. This redemptive intimacy with Levi had a ripple effect throughout the community of sinners. The friends of Levi saw in this shared meal a sign of their own acceptance. Those who fancied themselves to be without sins complained: "Why does he eat with such as these?" Their sinful alienation shut them out from such intimacy. Jesus made it very clear that he could call no one but sinners to salvation, shut out as he is by the self-righteous who have chosen to be on their own: self-contained and self-saved.

Jesus Saw Levi

...and Joe, Nancy, Lynn, Charlie, Pete, and Frances. He sees us all clearly. He sees tax collectors, workers in munitions plants, social climbers, aggressors in business, resentful parents, and the rebellious immature of whatever age. He sees all of this and much, much more. He sees followers.

That's the difference between our vision and Christ's. We get caught in the category trap, choosing to measure worth by what we do. It's the pharisee game: play by the rules and you are A-OK, you win. We like to be winners, so when it comes to self-scrutiny, the tendency is toward rule scanning. If we have kept the discipline pretty well, we are self-proclaimed winners. If there are too many infractions, we categorize ourselves as losers, and other pharisees are available to confirm the decision. Notice, the whole process is devoid of hope; you either "is" or you "isn't" in the winner's circle. But either way, self-saved or self-condemned, it's all the pharisee game: *you are on your own.*

On the other hand, Jesus does not judge by performance categories. He sees who we are, who we can be. He energizes potential, initiates the transformation of tax collector to apostle. His category is hope; we sinners are not left alone.

Levi Got Up

It takes at least that much initiative. We have to make the choice to change—not that we effect the changing but that we initiate the *choice* to change. That means getting up out of our self-designated roles (or holes) and letting Jesus lead us. Enlightenment happens when we look at the Lord, not at ourselves. The prodigal son already knew he was sitting in a pig sty, and Levi knew his part in oppression. Beating their breasts didn't get them on the road to life. They had to stop looking at themselves, rise up, and find the One who was waiting for them.

Similarly in the Rite of Christian Initiation of Adults, scrutiny and exorcism are not for wallowing in the garbage of our faults. They are rites for seeing the reality of our situation, for choosing to change, for getting up and for following. These rites offer the momentum to run the distance, to close the gap between myself and the Lord. Note that getting up also involves a repositioning. My relationship with everything around me will be different. The garbage that I step out of— money grubbing, self-pity, bitterness—is of no importance. What is terribly important is that my repositioning, my reorientation is to Christ and not to another self-centered rut. Catechumenate leaders, no less than anybody else, are inclined to confuse sin with sins. As a result, the period of purification and enlightenment can be misguided into a forty-day free-for-all for personal fault finding or, if the catechumenate team is of the same mind as my sin-rejecting liturgy planning friends, it can become glossed over as a forty day extended instruction, sprinkled with ashes and prayers of exorcism for the sake of doing the church thing. Neither of these fractured mentalities result in repositioning. What is needed is a wholistic under-standing of this stage of the journey. Enlightenment is no accidental companion to purification. Levi and his prodigal counterpart changed their way of life because of an inviting vision. Getting up is motivated by knowing a better place to go. "He got up and followed him."

Levi Got Up and Followed Him

Some phrases become so familiar and over-used that the original meaning drops out of them. This is one of them. To "follow Jesus" has been romanticized in song, sermon, and syrupy syntax right out reality. It has become bandwagon jargon that invites us to run, jump, and sing behind the rest of the folks for the sake of feeling good about the fact that we are a part of it all. Having lost sight of the leader, each simply follows the one in front in a mindless enterprise of mob spirituality. We Catholics are not exempt from that tempta-tion; we just go about it in a more orderly fashion than some. Still, we are prone to replace the leadership of Jesus with whomever happens to be in front of us. Some have been known to accept uncritically anything issuing from a throat encircled by a Roman collar, or, conversely, others leave the church because this or that priest has angered or scandalized them, forgetting that it is the Lord, not the priest, whom they are supposed to be following. Or some "forward-looking Catholics" may be inclined to follow just about anybody with a charismatic flair, while "traditionalists" are prone to ecclesio-latry, the worship of the church. All of these types have one thing in common: they have lost sight of *Jesus Christ as leader* and each one's personal responsibility as follower. The elect, and those on the threshold of the church, are no less susceptible to this trap. More often than not, it is the initiation ministers who unwittingly lead them into temptation.

The whole initiation process, and in particular the period of Purification and Enlightenment because of its intensity, is an environment ripe for guruism or institutionalism. Modern-day Christians are unused to the burden of much personal responsibility for their spiritual life. Catholics expect the church to tell them what to do in everything, fundamentalists expect the bible to be a compendium of daily decisions, and Christians of all sorts abrogate their personal responsibility by relinquishing it to their local minister. Let the church, the bible, or the clergy tell me what to do.

The problem in all these cases is the same: unwillingness to accept responsibility for my own life. It's the "do me something" syndrome. Obedience to the Spirit by deep listening to the Word of God, to the directives and wisdom of the church and to the Elders of our community is right, proper, and good common sense. But relinquishing responsibility for my life to anyone or anything except God is idolatry of one sort another. It could also be laziness, fearful faithlessness, ignorance or a combination of these and other assorted ills. To be a follower of Christ means exactly that. Conformity to an institutional church or to any one of its leaders, official or self-proclaimed, does not automatically assure conformity to Christ or to the way he lived out his life. Such internal configuration to Christ happens in the midst of a lived-out commitment to honest prayer and its insights, through which we gain a clear line of vision with the Lord, and because of which all other intervening agendas fall away. There is no shortcut to personal responsibility and commitment.

Purification and enlightenment, as the final preparation for public commitment to Christ, is preeminently a time of prayer: of listening to the one voice that says, "Follow *me*." It is vital that the elect be given the time and opportunity to hear that Voice; and that the hearing not be drowned out in the din of those who are busy filling up the bandwagon.

Jesus Sat at Dinner in Levi's House

Levi was converted from people oppression to apostle because the Lord ate and drank with him, because there was life-sharing between them. Through such intimacy dawned the nascent understanding of moral brotherhood. If sin and salvation are the structural dynamics of this Gospel story, redeeming relationship is the heart of it. Sin and salvation are meaningless mechanisms outside of relationship. The whole fabric of morality is inter-relational, good care-taking of one another in community (I am indebted to Timothy O'Connell's concept of morality as "good care-taking" in community, a concept he has expressed in various talks he has delivered). This is what Levi understood and what the pharisees didn't understand. Levi and his friends experienced redemption in life-sharing moments with Jesus, while the scribes and pharisees were too busy doing everything "right," too anxious about their score keeping to surrender themselves to another. Levi had no delusions about what he could do for himself. He simply brought the Lord into his house, and shared his table. Making room for the Lord in the house of our being is called prayer. It is not a pragmatic enterprise; prayer is not for *doing* anything, but for *being* with and allowing life and under-standing to flow between friends. Out of such moments of intimacy comes transformation and the holiness that issues in moral living.

Many Tax Collectors and Sinners Were Also Sitting with Jesus

Word sure got around fast! A horde of the local low-lifers correctly read in Jesus' choice of Levi their own preferential status at the kingdom table. They instinctively knew that the call of Levi was their own call as well. It's easy for sinners to understand their corporate connectedness. Besides, they felt at home with Jesus. He ate with sinners. There's no mistaking it, he identified himself with them. So when Jesus reclined at Levi's table, the whole thing turned into a social free-for-all. Literally free. "Come to the waters; / and you that have no money, come, buy and eat! / Come, buy wine and milk without money and without price" (Isa 55:1). There were no hoops to jump through either.

Come one, come all! If Jesus were running for election today, I'm sure his campaign buttons would be emblazoned with the insignia, "HCE: Here Comes Everybody!" Certainly that is one of the planks in the kingdom platform: Invite one sinner, invite 'em all. As his inviting and initiating church we must honor this. His church is not elitist—Christ invites not just selected sinners (those who polish up well); he invites *all* sinners. During this time when the elect will be scrutinizing the darker corners of life, it is especially important for them to feel the same freedom that Levi's friends felt: to know that the doors are wide open and all are invited to the table. The only credential required is to be "known as sinners." That is why we have scrutinies: to help us discern and admit our sinfulness. And because the Lord only calls sinners, scrutinies are bearers of good news.

The Pharisees Complained

Typical. We gripe about good news just because it isn't the news we are looking for. The need to be in control sure takes all the joy out of surprises. As a matter of fact, righteous folk tend to be grouches, sticks-in-the-mud, uptight and tiresome. They just can't see what is good news about being sinners. The Pharisees couldn't see any humor in it either.

It's deflating indeed to fight your way to the winner's circle only to find it full of losers. After all that hard work, discipline and self-polishing, the news that everybody is a winner just doesn't come across as "good." It's a reaction held in common by the elder son, the workers who bore the heat of the day, the pharisees on every occasion, and probably ourselves when we think about the "good thief" who stole heaven and all the other "thieves" in our own day who seem to be doing the same thing. It just isn't fair.

According to the dictionary, "complain" comes to us from the Latin, meaning "thoroughly beat." Not being a Latin scholar, my thoughts on this may be etymologically imperfect. But from human experience, it does seem that the complainer is one who is thoroughly beaten at his/her own game. By refusing to deal with reality, complainers are self-proclaimed losers. It certainly seems to be the case in this Gospel story. The pharisees refuse to *deal with the reality* that all their letter-of-the-law keeping has not justified them; rather it has made of them hypocrites and sinners of the worst sort. Because they cling to the fantasy of self-justification, they can not hear in Levi's call, their own invitation to the saving table. In their self-righteous-ness, they shut out the one and only savior around. And then they complain about it. The Lord explained elsewhere (Mk 8:35) the dynamics of this situation: those who seek to save their life will lose it; those who are willing to lose their life for the sake of Good News will save it. Like it or not, ready for it or not, the news is this: we are all sinners, and sinners have a savior, Christ the Lord. So what's to complain about? It sounds like good news to me.

It's pathetic how we fight it anyhow. Wouldn't you think that we would be *delighted* to delegate to Another the difficult (and for us, impossible) task of salvation? But no, we have to be in control even at the cost of great pain and terminal frustration. I remember a candidate who was extremely miserable because he couldn't learn enough fast enough, because his prayer wasn't "perfect," because he couldn't get his grown children to be "converted," and on and on through a long salvation list of his own making. In spite of assurances and counseling to the contrary, this candidate was unable to let go of his personal plan for salvation. He cut himself off from every open door and sat frightened and constantly complaining in his sealed world of do-it-yourself salvation. I suggest he is not a singular case. It is an epidemic temptation. You don't have to be self-assured to be self-righteous. Stubborn will do.

I Have Come to Call Sinners

If it isn't clear by now, here's one last chance to get it straight: Sinners can count on a savior; the self-saved count on themselves. Take your pick.

"God helps those who help themselves" is a half-truth the self-righteous use to justify their frenetic attempts to be their own saviors. It doesn't work. The Lord, who generally spoke in parables, said this in plain Hebrew: "I have come to call sinners, not the self-righteous." He who had unending patience and warm compassion for the bumbling masses cut off the self-righteous with cold precision: Hypocrites! Whited sepulchers! Brood of vipers! The sin against the spirit is deadly. Period.

Summing Up

As a paradigm for purification and enlightenment, the choice of this particular Gospel story may strike you as a poor second among other possibilities. Wouldn't a better choice have been the temptation in the desert or the text, "Come apart to a desert place and rest awhile"? Maybe. But my bias is that until we get our basic orientation straight, we'll never learn to pray or know where to look for help in temptation. This Gospel story sets that basic stuff straight: Jesus saves, sinners need salvation, Jesus came for sinners. If all of this is set straight, the whole business of purification and enlightenment begins to make sense. Certainly scrutinies and exorcisms are meaningless unless I accept for real the basic premise that I am a sinner. It's easy to fall into the old Lord! Lord!, thump-thump stuff that makes me feel *purged*, but doesn't touch a hair of my sinful self. Scrutinies are for touching the warm throbbing mass of sin alive and well in me, and for seeing it clearly. To admit that I am sinner is no pious concession; I'm wallowing up to my neck in sin!

That's enlightenment in its most fundamental form. It's the light bulb going on in the prodigal son's head: I'm sitting here starving in this pig sty while my father's servants are clean, clothed and fed. It is the light of anamnesis, the primordial remembering; it's the antidote for sinful amnesia, the rudimentary forgetfulness that we are children of a father who never forgets us. Enlightenment is the remembering of not only where we are, but who we are. Exorcism is throwing off the slop of my present infidelities in favor of the memory of a faithful father. Purification is the gift of being cleansed, robed and fed in my father's house.

Okay, why not choose the story of the prodigal son and be done with it? Well, that story is a great commentary on this whole issue, but it is only a parable. The incident with Levi isn't story time; it is about real people and real happenings. It concludes with a point-blank statement by Jesus about who is and who isn't called. It's vital stuff. I wanted you to take it seriously.

For Discussion

- Discuss RCIA 139's "a deeper knowledge of Christ." This period is about scrutinizing ourselves using the Scriptures as the tool. What do you understand to be the relationship of the law to life, particularly as Jesus presents it in the Scriptures?

- Who is the leader that you follow? How do you understand your responsibility to follow the "leader"? What is your understanding of "obedience to the Spirit"? How do you as a team define "morality"? What constitutes living a moral life?

- The reality is that everyone is a sinner. Jesus came to save sinners. Purification and enlightenment are for all—the whole community is involved as well as the elect and candidates. How does this impact our lives?

- In light of the discussion in "The Jesus Approach," what are foundational points that need to be present during this period? How is each present in your process?

The Rite Application

Very little is said in the rite about the period of purification and enlightenment. The whole thing is described on half a page. You might even say it is summarized in a single sentence: "For both the elect and the local community...the Lenten season is a time for spiritual recollection in preparation for the celebration of the paschal mystery" (RCIA 138). Lent is preparation for the paschal mystery; its entire meaning is interpreted in the light of the Triduum, the central celebration of the entire liturgical life of the church in which death and resurrection, baptism and Eucharist, sin and salvation all come together in redemptive resolution: the paschal mystery. This resounding experience of liberation reverberates through every Sunday of the year. We are told that preparation for this great celebration consists in interior reflection rather than catechesis. The elect are called to a learning of the heart, a deep interior process that opens the spirit to the vulnerability of life and death in Christ. This process of illumination is brought about by penance, by deep discernment of conscience, by the presentations of the Creed and the Our Father, and by the celebration of the Lenten liturgies.

Intense Spiritual Preparation

The rite uses these three intense words as a description of this period (RCIA 139). "Intense" derives from the Latin *intendere*, to "stretch out for." The period of purification and enlightenment pushes the elect to stretch out for new understanding and new vision, to break open the tomb of self-centeredness, and to pull away the last obstacles blocking the free passage of divine life. In the final preparation for dying in Christ, there is no room for complacency. Catechumenate team leaders must feel the urgency of the approaching mystery. There should be a fierce commitment in the air, a blue flame of purgation, light, and consummation. If the elect can't tell the difference between this period and the catechumenate, something is radically awry in the process and maybe even in the very life of the community itself.

"Intense spiritual preparation" is not the same as playing psychological games. Sometimes catechumenate teams go to great lengths to find something "different" to do with the elect during Lent. They send them on trust walks, give them clay to mold and hold, have them construct charts on the "tapestry of life," or subject them to any one of innumerable marketed plans of personal navel-gazing. These are supplemented with charming stories from quaint books like *Bag of Noodles* (Wally Armbruster [St. Louis: Concordia Press, 1973]).

The purpose of these stories of fantasy, I suppose, is to awaken our symbolic sensitivities in preparation for the Easter sacraments. Incredulously I wonder, "Why?" Why should we go looking for limping substitutes when we have before us the power of the Lenten lectionary and the robust symbols of fire, oil, death and stench, deep water, inbreaking light, fragrant bread, and heady wine? Why do some choose to use psychological exercises rather than to explore the extraordinarily powerful rites of the scrutinies and exorcisms? Why is fantasy substituted for the living tradition of faith and fidelity shared and gifted in the Our Father and Creed? When people arrogantly or ignorantly substitute their own pet projects and rites for those which have been tested through two thousand years of wisdom and experience, one fearfully wonders what bogus spirituality such a mentality transmits. I have found that those who are prone to impose their private spirituality in this way are also difficult to dissuade from doing so. At best, such obstinacy can only be explained by ignorance or fear of the robust intent of the Rite of Christian Initiation of Adults: radical conversion and baptism into the death of Christ.

Catechumenate teams that meticulously follow the "letter" of the rite can also fall into a trap. They may implement all the stages and celebrate all the rites, including the scrutinies and the presentations. But it is only slightly better than substituting the aforementioned irrelevancies if we present scrolls of the Creed and the Our Father just because it's neat to give out scrolls or because that's what you "should do," without even a nod to the deep tradition those texts embody or with little understanding of the sacred human ritual of handing on the tradition. Similarly, celebrating the scrutinies simply because they are there by-passes the enormous power these ancient rites can have for the profound conversion of the lifestyle and attitudes of the elect into the lifestyle and attitude of Christ.

The spirit of these rites underscores the conviction that prayer must certainly take priority during this period. We are told that the purpose of the period is to "enlighten the minds and hearts of the elect with a deeper knowledge of Christ the Savior" (RCIA 139). The stated object is knowledge *of* Christ, not knowledge about Christ. I know of no other way to accomplish this than by deep and consistent prayer. The forms of prayer are many; all types ought to be honored and encouraged during this time of intense spiritual preparation. Private prayer time can be enriched by including traditions of both quiet and vocal prayer. There are two forms of contemplative prayer. *Lectio divina* is a three-step method beginning with listening to a Scripture passage, which triggers reflection, affective prayer, and a state of rest in God. Centering prayer is a sort of shortcut to the third step, *contemplatio* (read Keating's *Open Mind, Open Heart* or the many publications on prayer by Basil Pennington). *Lectio divina* and centering prayer are reliable and perhaps indispensable means to a deeper knowledge and union with God in Christ. By way of introduction to contemplative prayer, the breaking open of the Word after dismissal could be approached in a more meditative manner, paving the way perhaps for a lifetime habit of *lectio divina*. Combining these contemplative forms with common devotions such as the rosary, stations of the cross, and holy hours before the Blessed Sacrament would provide a rich life of private prayer.

Liturgical prayer for the elect should not be limited to the Liturgy of the Word at Sunday assembly (or to the Easter sacraments for which they are preparing). The elect as well as the entire community should also have the opportunity to experience the Liturgy of the Hours. Lent is, in fact, the ideal time to re-introduce the whole parish to this ancient prayer of the church which has been lost to the laity for so long.

I realize that the celebration of the hours is not common practice in the parishes today; it is, in fact, rare. Vatican II's reformed breviary has failed to restore the hours to general practice within the church for a number of reasons, not the least of which is the prevailing attitude that the clergy, monks, and deacons are "commissioned" to pray the hours in the name of the entire church. But as Robert Taft points out, although we can and must pray *for* everyone, "no one can pray *in place of* anyone else, like some living prayer wheel that spins on vicariously while the world goes about its business" (362). Perhaps another reason that the Liturgy of the Hours has not caught on is that the form is monastic and not well suited to parish life. A more richly symbolic form, well established by the beginning of the fifth century is the so-called "cathedral hours." This ancient form "fleshed out the barebones of psalmody and prayer with rites and symbols that revealed the morning and evening hours as sacraments of the mystery of Christ" (348). Although this form was not restored per se by Vatican II, the spirit of the reformed rites encourages adaptation, and it is certainly within that spirit to introduce morning praise and evensong to the parishes in this form. It would certainly enhance the keeping of Lent for both the elect and the local community.

All other activities and busyness during Lent should give way to this primacy of prayer. Even almsgiving and fasting, named as important means of spiritual preparation, must never be seen as having independent or self-justifying purposes. The object of penance is interior clarity, a cleansing of the self-centered spirit. It opens one to a greater awareness of God in Christ and in one another. In other words, the object of penance is to pray always, and the object of prayer is union.

Purity of Mind and Heart

Today the relevancy of these rather quaint words seems to have passed with the usage of "thee" and "thou," and their meaning fossilized with the demise of the *Baltimore Catechism*. At best, our understanding of purity of mind and heart is generally limited to matters of the sixth and ninth commandments. But what did Jesus mean when he said, "Blessed are the pure in heart..."? (Mt 5:8). Another translation of this phrase is "single-hearted," a state of soul in direct opposition to what we call being "two-faced." Whom Jesus called "blessed" are those whose integrity commits them to the kingdom for its own sake rather than for motives of self-interest. In paragraph 139, the *Rite of Christian Initiation of Adults* weaves a connective thread between purity of heart, searching one's own conscience, and a deeper knowledge of Christ the Savior. The purpose of the scrutinies is to eliminate divisive elements in our lives, to become "single-hearted" in the love of Christ. Certainly for the elect, purity of heart and mind can be understood in terms of Romans 6:2: "How can we who died to sin go on living in it?" Here Paul echoes the undivided heart of the beatitudes, making it unmistakably clear that the unwholeness of sinful alienation is incompatible with life in the resurrected Christ.

Enlightenment

In the early church, baptism was called illumination, and the candidates for baptism were known as the *illuminandi*. This metaphor for baptism is suggested in Hebrews 6:4 and in this ancient hymn:

> Awake, O sleeper, and arise from the dead,
> and Christ shall give you light,
> the sun of the resurrection,
> begotten before the morning star,
> who gives life by his very own rays
> (Taft 350, quoting Clement of Alexandria,
> *Protrepticus* 9, 84:2).

The idea of enlightenment is more than a mental light bulb energized by instruction or catechesis. Instead, the illumination of baptism "is a burst of God's glory in those whose capacity to receive it has been expanded to their utmost" (Kavanagh, *Shape*, 119). Such a capacity has been fostered by fidelity in prayer, fasting, penance, alms-giving and thanksgiving. These things are what Christians do in faithful community. Enlightenment and purification are therefore invited not so much by catechesis and confession as by prayerful attentiveness. Illumination is a gift given to an undivided heart.

Processing the Process

Initiation is a complex, lengthy, and difficult journey. It requires a good deal of "processing the process." During this proximate preparation for the Easter sacraments, the elect are challenged to put all the pieces together and to focus their commitment to *really lean into* this Way of Christians. All this does not happen by magic.

It requires intense commitment, prayer, fasting, and a good dose of common sense. Good sense is not necessarily common among churchy ministers or the pious of whatever sort. In a fit of grandiose piety, some seem to think that handing over everything to the Spirit means abandoning common sense; assuming, I suppose, that because "the Spirit blows where it will," the use of good sense will somehow scare the Spirit away. The result can be that any random idea is imputed to be spirit-inspired. Consequently, sensible planning and solid human aids for good habit forming are ignored or even consciously rejected. The Holy Spirit is expected to take over as divine janitor and almighty entrepreneur all rolled into one, simultaneously cleaning up our messes and making all our enterprises successful. This attitude seems to be particularly prevalent among catechumenate teams during purification and enlightenment and also in mystagogia, probably because these periods move into territories quite undeveloped on the whole by American Catholics. We are terribly uncomfortable with constraints such as discipline, spiritual formation, practice of prayer, and painful scrutinies—and of such scary things as open-ended mysteries, the on-going call to holiness and the like. Thus we hope that initiation processes are magically formed and Christians are magically born, without need of too much team members' or candidates' responsibility in the matter. It doesn't happen. Kavanagh, quoting Tertullian, observed that Christians are made, not born (*Shape* 119). The Spirit is helped or hampered by human instrumentality and responsibility. All those aforementioned disciplines are necessary; furthermore we have to go about them with some awareness, intentionality, and good sense.

The human heart is terribly forgetful. We can find utter joy one minute and forget in the next moment how we came upon it. We are equally forgetful about the sources of our miseries. Journaling is one of those tools to help us remember our pains, our joys, and our insights into sources of both. It gives us the remarkable opportunity to record the history of our conversion journey, the unfathomable working of God in our lives. Journals also keep us honest; they allow us to step back from highs and lows at a more objective moment and scrutinize our motivations and judgments. We can record those wondrous and fleeting moments of clarity in which we stumble upon the core of essential questions. In spite of all these advantages, some catechumenate teams will not encourage journaling. Perhaps it is because they themselves have never journalized and therefore feel threatened by it; more likely, however, they are caught in the contagion of relativism that abhors upholding such a discipline, fearing that it might impinge on the elect's "freedom" to do as they please! Love, of course, does not leave us so free as to grant abortion of responsibility. It requires the discipline of getting to know the other and the self intimately. Journaling is a simple and effective tool for helping us know and remember.

Another method of "processing the process" is the retreat. Retreats are meant to provide the opportunity to stop, to identify who we are and who we are becoming. But it sometimes happens in initiation that retreats are turned into either fitness centers for spiritual calisthenics, revival camps for emotional frou-frou, or crash courses in self-analysis. A retreat ought not to be any of these. A retreat is literally a stepping back from our ordinary busyness in order to gain perspective. A retreat, like journaling, is a discipline. Discipline requires a letting go of one's own inclinations in favor of the way of another. Discipleship is the result. What is intended then, is the letting go of one's own agendas in favor of a clear focus on Christ. Spiritual muscle-building, emotional bulimia, or amateur psychoanalysis hardly have a clear christo-centric focus. What is needed is Scripture-based meditative time, various types of prayer opportunities (including contemplative forms), good liturgy, solid spiritual direction, and *stillness*. Even when a retreat is properly planned with all these good things, our American penchant for busyness tends to overfill the time. I know. I'm an inveterate perpetrator of over-kill. The hardest things to gift ourselves with are quiet time and personal space. But these are the classic gifts of retreat. "Be still, and see that I am God!"

For Discussion

- Read again RCIA 8. How does this impact the period of purification and enlightenment?

- Ordinarily, this period coincides with the season of Lent. How does the parish celebrate Lent? In what ways is this season different than all the others?

- Read briefly about the development of Lent. The emphasis on baptism has always been there but not always in practice. The catechumenal process reclaims this emphasis. The text also speaks of it as a time for spiritual recollection. What do you understand by this statement? In your process, is there a change in what you do or is it a time when you as a team panic because of "all that needs to be covered before Easter"? The text states that this period consists more in interior reflection rather than catechesis. On a scale of one (catechesis) to ten (interior reflection), where would you place your parish process. Why?

- The ritual text places emphasis on the need to purify one's mind and heart, to search one's conscience, and to do penance. In what ways are you enabling the elect to do this? It is the time to be *with* Christ rather than the time to learn more *about* Christ.

- In light of this discussion on purification and enlightenment, what insights have you gained? How might this insight impact your catechumenal process?

The Rite Mentality

The rites of this period are clearly the culminating preparations for the ultimate ritual of all: baptism into the death of Christ for the sake of resurrection in his life. Consequently, these rites are richly anthropological, perhaps more than previous ones. They invoke the great universal symbols and primitive intuitions of humankind: light and darkness, hunger and thirst, good and evil, destruction and death, freedom and life. They are gutsy and beautiful and deserve much more consideration than they are generally given. It is a sad commentary on the de-humanization of the church to say that many simply do not know how to relate to these basal human expressions. It is also clear that we have lost the deep sense of treasure and entrustment the people of God once had about the ancient texts of the Creed and the Lord's Prayer. The Rite of Christian Initiation of Adults presents the grand opportunity for us to recapture the value of all this once again.

The Skeleton Is out of the Closet

The ritual bare bones and backbone of this period are the scrutinies and exorcisms. It seems obvious from the names of these rites that the church is either linguistically fossilized or bound and determined to call forth unfaltering trust from the elect. Undergoing these rites requires a trust similar to placing one's life in the hands of a surgeon. We are told:

> The scrutinies are meant to uncover, then heal all that is
> weak, defective, or sinful in the hearts of the elect; to
> bring out, then strengthen all that is upright, strong, and
> good. For the scrutinies are celebrated in order to deliver
> the elect from the power of sin and Satan, to protect
> them against temptation, and to give them strength in
> Christ, who is the way, the truth, and the life. These rites,
> therefore, should *complete the conversion* of the elect...
> (RCIA 141).

One thing is certain. These rites are anything but insignificant. The burden of intention the church puts upon them is enormous: to discover and heal all that is weak, to uncover and strengthen that which is good; in a word, to complete the conversion of the elect! This tells us several things. First of all, the church takes the business of election seriously. Here are the chosen ones of God; the church is determined to present them to the Bridegroom spotless and without blemish. She is not afraid to confront the elect and call them to repentance, just as she calls the whole community to the real issues of conversion every Lent. Not content with pharisaic fasting and token sackcloth, but with prophetic courage the church proclaims true repentance:

> Is not this the fast that I choose:
> to loose the bonds of injustice,
> to undo the thongs of the yoke,

to let the oppressed go free,
  and to break every yoke?
Is it not to share your bread with the hungry,
  and bring the homeless poor into your house;
when you see the naked, to cover them,
  and not to hide yourself from your own kin?
(Is 58:6-7; see also the weekday lectionary, first reading,
Friday after Ash Wednesday).

With this same vigor, the church calls the elect to such honesty so that, as Isaiah goes on to say,

...light shall rise in the darkness
  and your gloom be like the noonday.
The LORD will...
  ...make your bones strong;
and you shall be like a watered garden,
  like a spring of water
(Is 58:10-11).

In order to accomplish all this, we are told plainly that *three* scrutinies are celebrated (not one or two) and that they should be celebrated within the ritual Masses, "Christian Initiation: the Scrutinies," which take place on the third, fourth, and fifth Sundays of Lent. The rite also plainly states that "the readings with their chants are those given for these Sundays in the Lectionary for Mass, Year A." Such very explicit instruction is not to be set aside lightly. But should some "unusual circumstances and pastoral needs" arise that requires purification and enlightenment take place outside of Lent, the scrutinies shall still be celebrated *in the same manner* (RCIA 146). The church, it seems, goes out of her way to say: You *shall* celebrate the scrutinies!

Whether or not the scrutinies achieve their purpose, however, depends largely on the sensitivity of two groups: the presider with the other liturgical ministers involved and the catechumenate team members who prepare for and unpack the rites for the elect. Such sensitivity is had only by those who themselves are open to self-searching and repentance and have an innate sense of human ritual.

The instructions for the scrutinies invite adaptation of the intercessions. Anyone who has involved the elect themselves in the discernment and naming of their own needs for scrutiny and exorcism can attest to the power of this kind of adaptation. When these self-named weaknesses and hopes for healing are prayed for and solemnized, the scrutinies truly uncover in *these* elect and in *this* community that which is weak, defective, or sinful. By their own self-searching, their real needs are surfaced and opened to healing. The elect and the whole community come face to face with the mystery of evil which really envelops our lives and into which Christ brings the hope of salvation. More than ever we understand the life and death issues of incorporation into Christ; with profound clarity we discover the meaning of sin and salvation.

The scrutinies carry the rhythm of the period of purification and enlightenment. Through the intercessions, the elect and the community with them, name the dark corners and stench holes of their living, and give them over to the power of the Almighty. "Lord, hear our prayer!" Then in a mighty invocation of the Trinity, the blackness is shattered and the rottenness washed away in the flood of the Spirit as the priest solemnly exorcises the elect. In a time when exorcism seems quaintly archaic or relegated to fright films, at a time when we have mystified evil right out of the real world or conveniently concentrated it in a camp labeled "they," the church has restored these ancient rites. Remarkably, they address our twentieth century world in a fresh and incisive way, calling us to confront not howling demons, but the real evil that honest men and women must encounter daily with courage. We are called to face that seductive, concrete, but often unconscious pull of the demons of our society that are part and parcel of our culture, our jobs, our neighborhoods, and of the very attitudes we live by. Such evil masquerades as "good sense" in the face of uncomfortable choices; it opts for saying prayers as an excuse for leaving justice undone; it is satisfied that "God helps those who help themselves" in the face of mass unemployment; it gobbles up world resources in the gluttony of "I earned it." In the midst of all this, the church proclaims healing, equity, truth, and freedom from the grasp of death, to which the people respond with a resounding "Amen!" "Amen!" "Amen!"

Rites of the Heart

"Amen" is our response of belief, our "credo." It derives from the Hebrew root *amin*, meaning "to be firm or sure," real, reliable, and valid (*Theological Dictionary* vol. 1, 232). It designates that to which we are willing to give our hearts. The Presentations of the Creed and the Lord's Prayer are rites of the heart, handing over as they do in the most loving and solemn fashion, our ancient treasures to the newest treasure of the church, her elect. They are given over for the sake of enlightenment and for the deeper realization of the spirit of adoption by which we can declare God, "Abba" (RCIA 147).

The rites of the presentations are extraordinarily simple, following a basic liturgical structure of readings of the Word with response, homily, the presentation, a closing prayer over the elect and dismissal. That which is most notable is that the elect are enjoined to *listen* while the community, led by the presider, passes on verbally the ancient treasure. Their response is a reverent and awed silence. Listening to the wisdom of the Ancient Ones, the elders of our tradition, is an art largely lost to our culture. But the hunger is still alive. In order to say, "Credo," "I give my heart to...," one must hear reverently and deeply the ancient wisdom.

Graciously the church gives the elect the ensuing few weeks to commit these treasures to memory, to orient their hearts and minds, and, through these filters of the Creed and the Lord's Prayer, to come to a place of fidelity. Then on the night of the great Vigil, in the company of their brothers and teachers, they shall publicly profess what they have come to treasure in unity with all the faithful.

Vigiling the Vigil

The preparation rites, so generally ignored, should probably be given a second look as a possible cure for the itch to rehearse the elect on Holy Saturday morning for the approaching Vigil. But whether or not a parish team chooses to celebrate these optional rites, three things are clearly recommended for the elect on Holy Saturday:

1. they refrain from usual activities,

2. they spend some time in prayer and reflection on the great mysteries before them, and

3. they observe a fast in so far as they are able (RCIA 185).

This is simply the way one keeps vigil. Remarkably, the inclination of some catechumenate teams is precisely the opposite: they enjoin the frantic activity of rehearsal, which is generally far from a prayerful experience, and they seem to want to feed them instead of fast them. Even those teams who clearly want to respect the vigil tend to fill it with "busy prayer-work." It is plain that we do not know how to vigil anymore.

Fasting is another lost art. Its cultural replacement is dieting. Ecstasy, the experience of moving beyond oneself, is replaced by self-control or, still worse, by narcissism. Barbara O'Dea, in her book *Of Fast & Festival*, suggests that fasting might be considered a religious equivalent of dieting (42). I really object to any conflation of these two concepts. The starting point, the abstinence from food, may be the same, but the objectives and motivations are very nearly diametric. That does not mean that dieting cannot be an essentially good and wholesome thing to do. Indeed, if one's health calls for it, it is the moral thing to do. But the object and motivation for dieting is the self; for fasting, it is the other. The intentional difference is self-control versus radical trust. The object of fasting is freedom, to be released from the tyranny of surface concerns so as to enter into the deep and real self where God abides. Its purpose is not penance but *kenosis*, the emptying of self-satisfaction, self-need, self-survival—for the sake of the riches of the kingdom. Fasting is another way to keep watch, a way to vigil, for the coming of the bridegroom. It combines in utter simplicity both purification and enlightenment.

For Discussion

- What is your present understanding of the celebration of the three scrutinies? How do you celebrate them in the parish? In what ways is the parish involved? How are the elect involved in the preparation of the scrutiny intercessions?

- How might you involve the parish more in the presentation of the Our Father and the Creed? Are these presentations celebrated during the purification and enlightenment period, or do you exercise the option of celebrating them during the catechumenate period? What would be some reasons for celebrating them in the catechumenate period?

- Do you celebrate the preparatory rites? Why or why not? In what ways do you invite the elect to prepare for the Vigil? Is fasting a part of the preparation? Why or why not?

- Are the elect encouraged to be present for Holy Thursday and Good Friday liturgies? Are they dismissed? Why or why not? There are differences in the practice of dismissal on these days. Some consider it all one celebration culminating in the Vigil, so they are not dismissed. Others dismiss the elect to reflect and pray together but no catechist is dismissed to lead them. It is important is to reflect on "why you do what you do."

Part Four

Sacraments of Initiation —
The Baptismal Mentality

"Immersion into mystery"

FOCAL ISSUES: death and resurrection

What Is the Baptismal Mentality?

> Do you not know that all of us who have been baptized
> into Christ Jesus were baptized into his death? Therefore
> we have been buried with him by baptism into death, so
> that, just as Christ was raised from the dead by the glory
> of the Father, so we too might walk in newness of life
> (Rom 6:3-4).

Baptism—the waters of death and the womb of regeneration (Fragomeni). It's true. Death and life are locked in a
single moment of transformation. Baptism is the prophecy of
the seed, the cross of contradiction, the reality of the *pascha*,
the passover. The paschal mystery is immersion into death for
the sake of undying life. Death and resurrection are the issues
we face when we incorporate into Christ.

Death has been treated as a vulgarity in our culture for years.
We don't talk about death in "polite company," and as a
nation we spend millions on formulas for eternal youth. A
woman in an ad for face cream sums it up: "I refuse to grow
old gracefully. I'm fighting it all the way." We lift and lacquer
our faces, drop pounds, pump iron, jog, and juggle physical
realities in an effort to obscure the approach of death. The

paradox of a society addicted to living is the sky-rocketing incidence of youthful suicide. The denial of death robs us of the possibility of exploring life's ultimate meaning. Baptism restores that possibility by reckoning with the reality that resurrection comes through death in the power of Christ.

Paul says clearly that we are initiated into death by participating, first of all, in *Christ's* death. To die with Christ means having the same attitude as Jesus: that of deep listening and perfect attunement to the Father, even at the price of ultimate self-surrender. Being of such a mind engenders a life of dying to, letting go of, security, the fear of obscurity, and the fear of failure. It means relinquishing the masks of youth and beauty, of strength and power. It means releasing the need to grasp at things of materiality and self-perpetuation so as to embrace the ultimate good of harmony and unity with the mind, the heart, and the will of the living God. All that high-flown verbiage makes our souls soar, but in the nitty-gritty of life it has the smell of death. These are the deaths that make physical dying look easy. It is the daily dying, not physical death, that kills us. Like Paul, we die daily to live in Christ, and death is gain. In preparation for the sacraments of initiation, we tend to up-play all the soaring and down-play all the dying. We do a disservice to the neophytes because in the long run, we must all face this daily dying with or without Christ. Without Christ it is simply death. But with Christ, there is pascha, passing through it all into the beyond of life. In Christ, we find death to be the seed of resurrection.

"We have been buried with him..., *so that*, just as Christ was raised...we too might *walk in newness of life*." Paul makes it very clear: death is for the sake of resurrection. The problem is that we understand resurrection no better than we understand death. Our addictive living forces us to translate "resurrection" as "resuscitation": a reconstituting of the old, a revival of the life we are so attached to. And so, instead of being an integral part of becoming alive, resurrection becomes something that happens after we die, our last bastion of hope should we finally lose the battle to survive. It is seen as our God-insurance for immortality (just in case we can't somehow discover it ourselves). Resurrection has become the Christians' mythology for the fountain of youth, *disconnected from the transformation of each moment of life here and now.* Interpreted as resuscitation, resurrection is impotent and without authentic hope.

Contrary to all of that, the initiatory sacraments and their promise of resurrection are not about self-perpetuation or insurance against final oblivion of life as we know it. Baptism, confirmation, and Eucharist are three moments of the singular life-death phenomenon of losing one's life for the sake of transformation into the corporate Christ. Transformation, a "crossing over" in form or essence, is about passage into a completely new way of being alive, as Paul says, a way that is radically different from and profoundly unsettling to an unredeemed view of things. In baptism, Christ is about the Father's business of re-creation "by laying waste our conventional certainties, undercutting our limitations in order to free us to pass through them and come out on their other side—as he himself passed through death into a life no one had ever lived before" (Kavanagh, *Shape*, 135). The initiatory sacraments are induction into that other-sided life through spiraling movements of death and resurrection that happen continuously throughout our physical life and beyond. These passages through death and resurrection are the ultimate issues of ordinary life whether we choose to face them or not. The sacraments of initiation are salvific in that they offer the possibility of transforming those daily, earthly struggles of ordinary life into divine encounters and all the deaths of life into victorious passages to glory in Christ Jesus the Lord.

All well and good. But the meaning of baptism is not revealed to a neutral bystander. By definition, sacraments are sacraments of *faith*. If Fowler is right, if faith is a way of leaning into life, then the sacraments demand much committed leaning. Such personal commitment is not accomplished by a magic dunking. We begin to glimpse what the pain of drowning in Christ might mean, and how the inbursting of the Spirit's breath revitalizes, only through days and years of grappling with death and with life. It does not come all at once; sometimes it never seems to come. It depends on our willingness to face with courage the basic issues of death and of resurrection. As Aidan Kavanagh so vividly proclaims: "When we are into initiation we are face to face with conversion in Jesus Christ dead and rising; and when we are into conversion in Jesus Christ dead and rising we are at the *storm center of the universe!*" ("Christian Initiation: Tactics and Strategy," my emphasis). The issue in initiation is this: incorporation into Christ is not a haven from storm; it is invitation into the storm's eye. Only by passing *through* the violent wrenching of the storm's spiraling forces can one reach its center of calm. Let us say so out loud and often.

Do You Not Know?

The Rite of Christian Initiation takes place at the Easter Vigil because no other time or liturgical celebration can speak so eloquently of these primal issues of life and death. This pivotal moment in the liturgical year brings together in word, symbol, and choreographed ritual all the cosmic forces in one sacramental moment of redemption. In the presence of fire, breath, beeswax, light and darkness, ancient stories told, water, nakedness and pure white robes, slick and fragrant oil running down, creed, candles and promises, shared bread and common cup—death and resurrection in Christ Jesus is made apparent in this our carnate world. Without these physical icons, the reality of redemption remains unmediated and merely suspected (Kavanagh, *Shape*, 135). Divine revelation has always been mediated through the material world: through burning bush and tablets of stone, thunder on the mountaintop and manna in the desert, cloud by day and fire by night, old ladies and virgins giving birth—and the Son of God made flesh. In full consciousness of this, the church throws wide open her treasure chest of rich symbols in revelation of the ultimate mystery of God, who died and rose for the re-creation of us all.

Not that we can or will absorb all this in a single sacred event. Nevertheless, the night of the great Vigil has the power to sacramentalize, to make present for us once again our human experiences of resurrection out of death; or we can allow it to become a deadly three-hour recitation of words, words, words, unimpassioned and devoid of the profound realities of death's stench and life's aroma. The power of the Vigil experience depends on two big Ifs: If the community and the elect have truly been caught up in a conversion process, and If the Vigil and the initiatory rites are done with hearty symbols, insight, and passion, only then does the church's song make sense:

> This is our passover,
> the night on which we are delivered...
> Tonight evil scatters,
> shame runs away,
> innocence blooms once more,
> we sing in our chains,
> we embrace in our fear,
> we kneel in deep quietude,
> we thrill in stillness.
> Heaven marries earth.
> We are clasped to God
> (Huck 74-75, paraphrasing the Exsultet).

Preparation Day

One certain way of killing all that for the elect and the catechumenate team is to rehearse on Holy Saturday. That's like a public announcement breaking into the middle of an inspired rendition of Beethoven's Fifth—a rehearsal on Holy Saturday is a blaring interruption of the concerted and single symphony of the Great Three Days. It would seem that the early church managed to have robust and transforming ritual without rehearsing the elect at all. Even so, if we cannot get along without it, let the rehearsal be before the Triduum, covering simply the practical logistics sufficiently to relieve undo anxiety and assure reasonable flow. Let nothing distract the faithful (including the initiation ministers) from the great event of the Great Three Days nor the elect from the holy Vigil. If anything is done with the elect on Holy Saturday, the preparation rites should be celebrated in a quiet meditative setting, providing anticipation for the great events of that evening. The rite is explicit: "The elect are to be advised that on Holy Saturday they should refrain from their usual activities, spend time in prayer and reflection, and, as far as they can, observe a fast. When it is possible to bring the elect together on Holy Saturday for reflection and prayer, some or all of [the preparatory rites] may be celebrated..." (RCIA 185).

In view of these clear directives, it is remarkable that some parishes persist in the practice of frantic activity, busy rehearsals, and even festive anticipation of the initiatory sacraments by throwing a party or having a luncheon for the elect on Holy Saturday! Such activities are in complete contradiction of the directives of the rite and show a total lack of understanding of the Triduum itself. But strangely enough, such abuse is common on Holy Saturday even by catechumenate teams otherwise well informed and apparently in tune with the process. Rehearsal on Holy Saturday arises out of a common need for organizing logistics and a legitimate concern for good liturgy. A certain amount of rehearsal may be necessary for sanity and for an unobscured message to the assembly who, unlike the Christians of old, haven't a clear idea of what is going on. But nothing requires the rehearsal to take place on Holy Saturday, and over-rehearsal tends not to clarify but to render profane the sacred rituals. I have actually seen rehearsal carried so far as to have a practice "dunking," and with such bad taste as to call it a "wet T-shirt contest!" I mention this grotesque example to illustrate how far we sometimes go to create a comfort level for ourselves or others. Secularizing the sacred takes all the scariness out of it (as if we should be comfortable approaching divine epiphanies). But such a shallow and ribald attitude is offensive and incomprehensible and tends only to perpetuate the equally offensive mentality that baptism by immersion is unseemly, or at least "non-Catholic." These two extremes of profanity and prudery arise out of the same self-centeredness that seeks to protect ourselves against personal vulnerability to the symbolic, deeper realities.

An excellent tool for opening oneself to the deep mystery of the divine inbreaking is the ancient discipline of the fast. Moreover, compliance with the rite and the spirit of good vigiling calls for the paschal fast to be encouraged and upheld. Violating the paschal fast seems to arise out of an ignorance of its very existence. The clergy itself seems unaware of it. It is rare to hear the paschal fast recommended from any pulpit. Yet the documents of the church clearly call for a fast from after the Holy Thursday liturgy until the Easter Vigil (see *Constitution on the Sacred Liturgy* 110; *General Norms for the Liturgical Year* 20; RCIA 185; for the spirit and theology of fasting, see Paul VI's apostolic constitution *Paenitemini* [*Penance*] [1966], chapter 3). It is simple enough to extend the Good Friday fast through the vigiling of Saturday. The problem, perhaps, is that the Good Friday fast is regulated by church law, whereas the Easter or paschal fast (which includes both Friday and Saturday) is urged but not commanded. Does the general silence about the paschal fast indicate that our pastoral leadership is still caught in the throes of legalistic piety? Or is such silence the result of blatant ignorance? Either way, it betrays a certain insensitivity to the deeper aspects of sacramental spirituality. Openness to the great mysteries of our redemption requires the free plunging of ourselves, body and spirit, into the tomb, so that through union with Christ buried we may be united with him also in resurrection. Fasting of the physical organism symbolizes the relinquishment of our clinging need to survive. It unites us to the obedience of Christ in full view of crucifixion. It opens our bodies as well as our spirits to the glory of Easter resurrection. What further reason do we need? Take the plunge. Observe the paschal fast.

Plunging Deeper: Cult versus Sacrament

If the liturgical renewal instituted by Vatican II has done anything, it has shaken our Catholic self-understanding from surface to core. Some of the practices, postures, and language we used to think of as the "essence" of Catholicism have disappeared. If that is not distressful enough, there seems to be a growing ritual commonality between Catholic and some forms of Protestant liturgy. I cannot count the number of times I have heard the comment about some "modern" Catholic practices: "It's too Protestant for me!" or "I feel like I'm in a Protestant church." (More often than not, these comments are voiced by those who have never set foot inside a Protestant church!) What these people are really saying is that they have identified their life of a Catholic Christian with non-essential externals which, rather than giving them a positive identity with Christ, simply separated them from the "other guys." Now, without these badges of identification, they do not know who they are or what their spiritual life is in fact all about. Without these externals they can't tell themselves apart from the rest of the world, a world which they have cavalierly labeled "Protestant." The underlying issue is a serious one. It is the substitution of religion for spirituality, of cult for sacrament.

In his book *The Call to Conversion*, Jim Wallis recounts a true story that describes this same phenomenon among evangelicals. During high school, he was dating a girl of an evangelical faith. Although movie-going was frowned upon by evangelicals, he thought it was safe to invite her to see *The Sound of Music*. To his astonishment, the girl's father physically blocked her way and passionately proclaimed: "If you go see this movie, you will be trampling on *everything we believe* and have *raised you to be*" (24-25, my emphasis). Wallis notes that the father's intense reaction to this rather benign movie betrayed the undergirding reality of his surface concerns. Deep in his soul that father knew that these certain externals *were*, in reality, symbolic of the few fragile barriers left that distinguished them from the un-Christian world. And so he felt compelled to resist this final encroachment of the secular into his Christianity: a Julie Andrews movie. Catholics who cling to the idea that "everything we believe is being trampled on" by the removal of altar rails, religious habits, Latin songs, and bells at Mass may as well picket *Sound of Music* too. Such mentalities all have the same root, and it isn't exactly the heart of the Gospel. It is, in fact, a way to *ignore* the heart of the Gospel (which demands painful change, the doing of justice, and self-relinquishment) by giving one's heart instead to some simple, manageable externals which allow us to remain essentially unchanged. It is a way to feel justified without personally doing justice, a way to claim righteousness without having to relinquish selfish satisfaction.

I mention these things here because when it comes to the Easter sacraments, the issue is invariably raised (not usually by the elect but by a Catholic) that baptism by immersion seems too "Protestant." The real discomfort, of course, is that baptism by immersion moves us in one wet instant out of our neat in-control "Catholic" world and immerses us into the messy and multiform possibilities of what baptism might demand. "Aha!" someone objects. "A 'conservative' clinging to a dainty dribble is no worse than 'modern' insistence on a demanding dunk. Either way, you are hanging the meaning of your religion on a ritual!" Exactly. It is the meaning of the ritual action we are after here. That's what sacraments are all about. Our sacraments are not in the same category as movies, vigil lights, religious clothing styles, or Latin chants. Sacraments enact the poignant memory of who we are as Christians and who we have been called to become. We don't baptize to feel safe about the baby (or ourselves) or to pay our religious dues. We baptize in order to publicly surrender to the God-covenant already drawing us into a relationship that is continually transformative. All symbolic, sacramental activity is like a kiss; it is a primal statement of how we really are in relationship with the Other (distant or intimate), and how we do it *this time* changes or reinforces our understanding of that relationship.

That being the case, what statement does a dribble of water say about the baptismal life, and what does immersion into a pool of running water say? A trickle of water says: "My relationship with You and Your people is minimal, not too scary, and is guided by matters of convenience. It does not require me to be naked or vulnerable. It is possible to sleep through it. Symbolically, a trickle of water leaves me basically unchanged, largely unwashed, and rather complacent."

Immersion says differently: "My relationship with You and Your people can be inconvenient and scary and requires me to be deeply connected to this carnate world. It puts me in a position of extreme vulnerability: nakedness, breathlessness, and even looking into the face of watery death. It also leaves me clean and refreshed, sucking in new breath, alive and full of adrenaline; it leaves washed away in the pool all the pretenses of who I am before the world. And it is impossible to sleep through it."

The difference between cult and sacrament is that the first is designed to satisfy our need for religion; the second is designed to call forth self-transformation.

The Sacraments of Initiation

It is not within the scope of this book to offer an in-depth look at the initiatory sacraments, but honesty demands that we not bypass a glimpse into the challenging spirituality to which these sacraments call us. First of all, incorporation into Christ is an incarnational affair. The very term "incorporation into Christ" is incarnational; Christ is the Word made flesh, and by incorporation into Christ we are talking about forming the fleshly body of the risen Christ, sharing the same life, being connected as member to member. Which, of course brings us to the second essential quality of Christianity: it is by its very nature communal. This is not open to personal opinion. It is impossible for many members to belong to a single body and not be essentially communal. The third element of Christian spirituality is that we are sinners made whole. Jesus Christ alone has conquered death and brought flesh and spirit into redeemed unity. Finally, incorporation into Christ is a graced relationship; that is, we live by a life that transcends us, which is the Spirit of God.

The celebration of the sacraments, especially those we call initiatory, must speak to these essential Christian concepts. If these sacraments are celebrated in the midst of an unconcerned or self-absenting community, what does this say about the corporality and communality of this body? If those who have no personal connection to those being received into the church feel no pull to stand vulnerable before the mystery of the dying and rising Christ in our midst, is it because we do not know we are sinners gifted with the Spirit who alone can make us whole? Do we presume to have already "made it"? Do we presume that we can be saved by ourselves? Once we are initiated, do these sacraments have nothing more to say to us? Such attitudes bespeak a desacralized people deformed by a non-sacramental spirituality. The church, in the *Constitution on the Sacred Liturgy*, makes this proclamation, often quoted but perhaps seldom really heard:

> The liturgy is the summit toward which the activity of
> the Church is directed; at the same time it is the fount
> from which all the Church's power flows....The liturgy...
> moves the faithful, filled with "the paschal sacraments,"
> to be "one in holiness" (*Roman Missal*, prayer after
> communion, Easter Vigil); it prays that "they may hold
> fast in their lives to what they have grasped by their
> faith" (*Roman Missal*, opening prayer, Mass for Monday
> of Easter Week); the renewal in the eucharist of the
> covenant between the Lord and his people draws the
> faithful into the compelling love of Christ and sets them
> on fire....Grace is poured forth upon us as from a
> fountain (10).

The document elaborates on the necessary conditions for this power, in the very next, but less quoted, breath:

> But in order that the liturgy may possess its full
> effectiveness, it is necessary that the faithful come to it
> with proper dispositions, that their minds be attuned to
> their voices, and that they cooperate with divine grace,
> lest they receive it in vain (see 2 Cor 6:1). Pastors must
> therefore realize that when the liturgy is celebrated
> *something more is required than the mere observance of the
> laws governing valid and lawful celebration*; it is also their
> duty to ensure that the faithful take part fully *aware of*

what they are doing, actively engaged in the rite, and enriched by its effects (11, my emphasis).

Christian spirituality is at its very essence sacramental. The incarnation of the Son of God made that an incontrovertible fact. We must attend to it.

Immersion into Mystery

The sacraments of Christian initiation are not a finale to a year of preparation. They are the final preparation for embarking on a lifetime of conversion. We cannot say that often enough. We certainly do not believe it enough. With good will all around, catechumenate teams year after year, parish after parish, graduate rather than initiate. It is human fragility. On-going conversion is demanding; we would rather look for signs of completion, of success, of having arrived.

But as we have seen throughout this book, there is no such thing as having arrived. Though an apparent disappointment, this is, in fact, the great hope inherent in life: there is always more to enliven us. The secret of a mystery is not that it is unintelligible but that there is no limit to its revelation. Immersion into the mystery of Christ engages us in the unlimited possibilities of life.

There are three sacraments of initiation. All three invite into immersion of one sort or another. The first two sacraments drown us in Christ and in his Spirit. The third is the ongoing process of God's immersion in us. These three processes are inseparable and never ending. Thanks be to God!

For Discussion

- Discuss your understanding of the sacrament of baptism. How has your understanding changed and/or deepened and/or expanded over the years? What has prompted this change?

- Read the section of St. Paul's letter to the Romans that is proclaimed at the Easter Vigil. Discuss the implications of this Scripture reading.

- Recall Passover experiences in your own life and in the life of the parish. What was/is the transformation taking place? How is such transformation connected to the paschal mystery?

- It behooves your team to return to this section over and over again. It is foundational to the whole process. Without continued dialogue on this topic of baptismal mentality, your process can become just another parish program controlled by a few people and done to those who want to become Catholic. What you are engaged in is "immersion into the mystery of Christ."

Part Five

The Mystagogical Mentality

"Leaning into life"

FOCAL ISSUES: sacrament and mission

What Is the Mystagogical Mentality?

> Now on that same day two of [the disciples] were going
> to a village called Emmaus, about seven miles from
> Jerusalem, and talking with each other about all these
> things that had happened. While they were talking and
> discussing, Jesus himself came near and went with
> them... (Lk 24:13-15).

N ow we're into familiar territory. We know this road—it's
our road. Mystagogy is about living and understanding
the baptismal life; it is the Catholic Christian endeavor.
Hurrah! That's what a lot of us have been working at all our
lives. Mystagogia is no mystery to us! "Uh-huh, sure!" you
say. "Then how come, out of all the periods of the initiation
process, mystagogia is definitely our Waterloo?" It's true.
Mystagogia is the last thing to come and the first thing to fall
apart, not just because we are tired but because, in all honesty,
we don't know what to do with it and the trivia we fill it
with invites boredom. Have we, in the last analysis, brought
these people through nine months, a year, two years, or more
of intense preparation for entrance into a life about which we
have nothing to say? A life with which we are bored or about

which we are so ignorant or have so little experience that we have nothing to share? It is a frightening question. To ask it does not mean the worst is true. But surely we must ask ourselves, at least for our own benefit, why it is that we find it so difficult to touch and share the mysteries of our Christian experience. The issues at stake in mystagogia are sacrament and mission; why are these issues so intangible?

If we are out of touch with mystagogy, there is a good chance that we are out of touch with life, with that deeper aspect of it we call the mystery of life. That's no big news. In our helter-skelter world crammed with work, work, work, money worries, frustrations of time and purpose, social and political dishonesties, and frantic play, it is no surprise that the "things unseen" are left unseen. In a world in which we are measured by what we do, what we own, and whom we control, there is little encouragement to explore the world of being. Strangely, we nevertheless know that only in this deeper place can we find meaning and purpose. It is through encounter with the sacred in the ordinary passages of life that we begin to understand. The Emmaus story is that kind of encounter.

On their way to Emmaus, the disciples were trying to sort out everything that happened in the last three days and over the last three years. They were having a hard time of it. On the face of things, nothing made sense. Then Jesus fell in with them; in the guise of a stranger and in the symbol of broken bread he was made present to them. Through this sacramental, symbolic mediation they discovered hope, clarity, faith, enthusiasm, and the courage to witness. Emmaus is the apostolic story of mystagogy: the unveiling of and joyful witness to the mystery and promise of Christ, dead and risen, *through the carnate presences of earth*. The door to Christian mystagogy is openness to the sacramental, to the inner reality of outward signs; it is willingness to be invested in the symbolic rituals of life. And for us no less than the apostles, such sacramental experience gives birth to a sense of mission, of joyful witness.

Unfortunately, many Catholics have inherited either a mystified or a mummified understanding of sacrament which invests it with magic power or divests it from meaning altogether. It is no wonder. Before the renewal of Vatican II, the church's attitude about sacramental ritual was severely reduced to concerns of matter and form, to simply "getting the job done." Whether or not the persons involved *understood* what was done or whether they were personally invested in the sacrament became less and less important. It was that familiar trap of *doing* to the detriment of the deeper sense of *being*. We came very close to regarding our sacraments as magical zaps of membership, cleansing and feeding, rather than conduits of divine life rooted in the things of human life. A clinical understanding supplanted a sense of the symbolic.

But nothing sacramental can be understood without a robust sense of simple and earthy symbols. When people complain that we have lost a sense of the sacred in our liturgies, what they mean is that our ritual is devoid of door-opening symbol for them. Indeed our whole culture is symbol poor. Our industrialized world has become so domesticated and pragmatized that we have lost sensitivity to the significance of earth and her primal symbols. Thus Gerard Manley Hopkins so eloquently lamented:

> Generations have trod, have trod, have trod;
> And all is seared with trade; bleared, smeared with toil;
> And wears man's smudge and shares man's smell: the soil
> Is bare now, nor can the foot feel, being shod
>
> ("God's Grandeur," *Poems of Gerard Manley Hopkins*, 4th ed.,
> W. H. Gardner and N. H. MacKenzie, eds. [London: Oxford
> University Press, 1975]).

We the church, no less than the world, have forgotten how to stand barefooted before the great theophanies our sacraments incarnate. Robust symbolic activity, which by its very nature would break open for us emotionally charged meaning that seduces into commitment and transformation (Empereur 43), had been domesticated into merely functional signs offering little more than discipline and definition. Through the restoration of good ritual and fuller liturgical symbols, Vatican II initiated the recovery of a sacramental spirituality within the church. But it takes more than renewed ritual. It takes "symbolizers," *people of wonder,* who, like Alice, are willing to pass through the looking glass, to lean into life, to risk the surprising, to be caught by ecstasy, to be crazy enough to buy the whole field for the sake of a single, priceless pearl. Throughout this book, I have tried to open up this mentality. Initiation calls for ministers who are symbolizers of the sacred. For a mystagogue, it is a way of life. We depend on mystagogues, as we depend on poets such as Hopkins, to name the theophanies in life:

> The world is charged with the grandeur of God.
> It will flame out, like shining from shook foil;
> It gathers to a greatness, like the ooze of oil
> Crushed....

Mystagogy is the grappling with the experience of mystery, the discovery of the sacred in the heart of the profane. This is the ultimate question of human life. In the final analysis, the inner promise of transcendence rescues human life from absurdity. When the sacred slips into our helter-skelter journey through human days, we, like the disciples on the way to Emmaus, experience a heartening, a sweet illumination, and eventually the redeeming celebration of the mysterious union of God and man. We come to know God—in a sacramental moment.

Sacraments are not magic. They are redemptive and graceful if we attend to them because they invite us into deeper reality, illuminating the mystery of God veiled but already present in human life. Sacraments are necessary, not because the church says so but because ultimately human life demands transcendent meaning. Mystagogy is fundamentally a sacramental adventure, an invitation into deeper meaning. Mystagogues discover that meaning, savor it, and then shout it out to all who will listen—which brings us to the other mystagogical issue, mission.

Mission, resting as it does on sacrament, is no less misunderstood, no less tainted with the functional and the pragmatic. We get it all balled up with ministry that has us running around like Martha, "doing" things, especially churchy things. And like Martha, we are also inclined to invoke the Lord to commandeer the neophytes into the same busyness. We do it every year during mystagogy, thinking that we have produced only half-baked Catholics if we don't get them to "sign on the dotted line" for some parish ministry. I hate to be the bearer of bad news, but ministry is not what constitutes Christians.

Ministry is a designated role; it is a particular way, out of many ways, by which one serves one's constituents. Ministry defines function; mission delineates purpose. In jargon, mission is our goal; ministry helps us strategize that goal. The Christian mission is to fulfill the promise of the kingdom: to live justly and caringly as Jesus lived, to love tenderly and wisely as Jesus loved, and to walk as Jesus walked—humbly before his Father. In a word, the Christian mission is to sacramentalize Christ to the world. Without this deeper understanding of mission, ministry is just a job. Mystagogia is about *mission*. It is about believing and proclaiming and living out the incredible news that God incarnated, that we are not abandoned, that death is done in, and that life is new. Not limited to the confines of a particular role, mission encompasses a lifetime kaleidoscope of varied moments of clarity and multiple ways of divine encounter. Mission is a gut response to this fractured realization that we are loved, redeemed, and renewed. Mission happens when, after difficult and painful passages, we recognize the Lord and run back in the night to give witness to Christ alive.

Our difficulty with mystagogia is not that we are bored with Christianity but that we are bored with the insignificant and the shallow which have replaced the sacramental in our lives. The doing and the accomplishment of things have preempted the inner challenge of being; control and manipulation stand in the place of risk-taking presence. In order to get in touch with the sacred, we must be willing to be vulnerable, to invest ourselves in direct encounter with the sacramental moments of our everyday lives, and to risk the revelation of mystery. Nobody graduates from mystagogia. (When is anyone ever sufficiently immersed in the mystery of Christ?) It is our endeavor no less than the neophytes'. Nevertheless, the question before us as ministers of initiation is: How can we facilitate this part of the journey for the newly baptized? The issues we must struggle to come to terms with are sacrament and mission. The underlying realities are the meaning and purpose of Christian life.

For Discussion

- What are you presently doing for this period? Why? How is what you do different than the other three periods?

- What do you understand to be the goal of this period? On a scale of one (avoiding drop-outs) to ten (integration into the community), where is your process? Why do you place your process there on this continuum?

- Mystagogy is not some contrived experience to "keep" the neophytes. It is a natural phenomenon that follows any heightened experience, that is, to talk about the experience and to glean the insights and/or truths of the experience. Mystagogy is a gradual unfolding of the meaning of baptism and what it means to be a disciple of Christ. It is a lifelong period. You are still in this period. You are still learning what your baptism is and means.

• What is the place of sacraments and mission in your lives and in the life of the community?

The Jesus Approach

As we have noticed, there is something about mystagogia that seems out of reach, beyond our experience. Because mystagogia is post-baptismal catechesis, it may very well be beyond our experience because many of us can't remember our baptism or when, if ever, we *consciously* began to unpack its meaning. Mystagogia is scary for most catechumenate team members because we, like the disciples on their way to Emmaus, are still trying to sort it all out for ourselves. Perhaps that is why the Emmaus story is one of our favorite Gospel stories. We can really relate. We find ourselves in the disciples' shoes over and over again. But as an initiation minister, it is time to approach from a different direction, to slip into the shoes of Jesus, to see the process from his perspective. As a model for mystagogy, there is no Gospel segment more apropos than the Emmaus story.

Here are two sincere men who have truly discipled Jesus. They have left their accustomed ways, heard his word, and followed in his footsteps. Doing so has not led to glory but to death. They really hadn't bargained for that. What is this Christ *really* all about? Where do they go from here? Still unwilling to admit a crucified Christ, they head out of Jerusalem. Joining them in their journey, the crucified and risen One offers them a presence they could admit, deal with, and find meaning in. Because they experience him in a new and sacramental way, they can join the community of believers.

In the light of this, what would be the "Jesus approach" to neophytes in the throes of mystagogy? Well, according to the story, he would find the road they are on, get in rhythm with their step, and accommodate himself to where they were at. He would not assume that because it is Easter day that life has magically changed for them. These disciples have gone through a traumatic experience; they may be distressed about all the things that happened in the last three days. He would ask them, "What things?" which would allow everything to come tumbling out. Then he would open the Scriptures and break bread with them.

Two of Them Were Going

Whatever their historic motivation was for this trip, the symbolical message is clear: these two disciples put their backs to Jerusalem and made tracks out of there. They definitely had the feeling it was all over. In spite of the joy and euphoria of the Easter sacraments, the feelings of the neophytes may, at times, not be so different from those of these disciples. True, the neophytes know Christ is alive and well "out there." But whether or not they perceive Christ alive and well in their lives is another question. Feeling alone and uncertain is not an unusual experience for neophytes. Many unconsciously put distance between themselves and the company of the faithful in order to buffer the unspoken and even unrecognized pain of utopia undelivered or of their own as yet imperfect understanding.

When we see neophytes heading down roads that seem to be going in the wrong direction, are we tempted to blockade the road, insisting on it being a one-way street? Or do we decide that we have done all we can, shrug our shoulders, and let them go? Jesus did neither. He accompanied them, walked a long way with them, helped them get in touch with what really happened, was present to them, and then left them with the gift of self re-direction. As a result, they returned joyfully, owning the faith they witnessed. Grabbing them by the hair of the head and dragging them into ministry is slightly less effective.

While They Were Talking and Discussing

There is no doubt that the disciples had *plenty* to talk about. The hopes, dreams, hard work, and generous service of the last three years didn't quite get them where they thought they were going. Worst of all, they had lost their leader, the hope of the nation, and their dearest friend. Just about every basic life issue was turned upside down. An intense reaction was predictable. It was simply not possible to dismiss the whole thing with an "Oh, well!" and a shrug of the shoulders. They needed some time to talk it out, to find meaning.

Reactions can tell you a whole lot about the quality and intensity of an experience. But reaction and reflection require the luxury of time and space to recall and touch the experience. Ministers who expect to call forth reactions have to offer those two luxuries. The Lord let the disciples walk a while by themselves and express a lot of frustration before he even got into the act. This gave them the opportunity to identify their experiences and to name the gaps in their understanding of discipleship. Jesus also had the good sense to fall in step with them, to listen to their story, and to take his cue from them. As Americans we have a difficult time doing that. We like to set the pace and imprint our pattern; we don't listen very well. We are too busy doing and telling. As initiation ministers we are tempted to be busy, busy, busy instructing, molding, pushing, and prodding. Whatever experience the neophytes have had may get buried below the pile of activities we bulldoze into their laps.

Tom Caroluzza compares mystagogia to the time needed for debriefing people after a highly emotional and intense experience such as being held captive by terrorists, being a prisoner of war, and having just been married! The point is that, after a peak experience of whatever sort, folks need ways to relate that experience and their new attitudes to ordinary life. Experiences that shake up life take a lot of debriefing. Neophytes need time to ease into the common life of the church. Christian initiation is not a rescue-and-dump operation. Wisely, the American church has extended the debriefing time of mystagogia to a full year (*National Statutes for the Catechumenate* 24). Now we can afford to take the great fifty days to tap into the Easter mysteries. That still gives us lots of time to commission these folks into the ordinary ministerial life of the church.

Intense experiences are most likely to generate lively reactions. If, given the right circumstance and opportunity, the neophytes' reactions are less than lively, it may indicate that not much of significance happened in the catechumenate. If that is the case, there isn't a whole lot the catechumenate team can do to make mystagogia meaningful. Meaning cannot be applied like ointment but is locked in the heart of experience. Ray Kemp says it in plain English: "Mystagogical experience is in direct proportion to our conversion experience, our rising only as true as our dying" (54). The sobering truth is that resurrection is not an automatic pleasure form; it is always preceded by the distress of death and always makes demands of the new life it engenders. The flower of Easter has roots in the deep soil of death and conversion. There is no easy access to resurrection—not for the disciples, not for the neophytes, not for anyone. If we don't have the nerve to dig deep in the catechumenate, the harvest at Easter is likely to have shallow roots.

What Things?

"What things?" is a mystagogue's question, and questioning is a mystagogue's method. Jesus could have told them everything they were thinking, but instead he gave them the opportunity to touch their own experience. Faith may be a gift, but coming to faith is definitely a participatory operation. Not even Christ could force its fruition.

It does help to talk things out with someone who has been down the same road, who knows where it goes. It is an important catharsis for folks just to get things off their chest. Sometimes it is difficult to get in touch with our experiences until we try to communicate them to others. Neophytes may not even realize that their lives have been upended until they try to express the past year's goings-on. And like the two disciples, recounting it all may still not bring immediate understanding. But one thing is certain. Unless the question (what things?) is raised, the mystery cannot be explored.

"What things?" is a sacramental question. For the disciples the sacramental things were nails and crucifixion, perfumed spices, burial windings and rolled stones, empty tomb and wondering words, fellowship and broken bread. Him they did not see. But the things they did see and hear were gateways to the Christ they could not see. And so with us today, "What things?" is also a sacramental question. It evokes deep remembering of darkness and burning light, ancient words and waters of death, new gasping breath and white robes wrapped, fragrant chrism rolling down, community bread and heady wine. Him the neophytes do not see. But in these things, they too unveil Christ if we let them.

We Had Hoped

They had hoped that he would set them free. In spite of all the information they had gleaned during their "catechumen-ate," in spite of the eyewitness testimony of the women that Jesus had indeed risen, the two disciples were still hard pressed to believe the good news of freedom and salvation. Life pushed hard upon them.

Christ broke the bonds of death on the third day. It takes a bit longer for the rest of us. Conversion only happens little by little and on multiple levels. Layer by layer we shed the old self; season by season we become a new creation. The Easter Bunny does not bring resurrection in a plastic egg. The jolt of mystagogia is the realization that the Easter Vigil is not graduation but induction. "O LORD, you have enticed me, / and I was enticed" (Jer 20:7). Now it all begins in earnest. The honeymoon is over, but learning to live in union and service is before us still.

Hope is perhaps the cardinal virtue, the hinge, of mystagogia. While faith leads to incorporation, hope gives the courage to live it out. But it is impossible to have hope if I am under the impression that it is all done and over with. If our "newly planted" die on the vine, it may be because the community or at least its ministers present a closed, packaged deal for salvation. As if it were a commodity, salvation is packed and proselytized—full satisfaction guaranteed. But the neophytes don't find themselves satiated. They bought the "package," but death is still around. Now they are trudging down the road away from Jerusalem. Hope fades fast on the heels of false advertising. Hope is also a tough virtue to maintain and understand in a world of immediate gratification. It is difficult for us to steer clear of the "salvation vending syndrome"; salvation is auctioned off on television every day. Maybe one day these hucksters will be sued for false advertising. In the meantime, buyer beware! More importantly for the church, vendor beware! The reign of love is near but not yet here; the need for faith and hope has not yet passed away.

Jesus never offered a panacea. He kept warning his followers about their false hopes and political interpretations; he kept telling them that death and passage to an unknown life was in the offing, that the way is rough. But he also opened before them a kingdom of hope, a whole new world of possibility. So when in their pain he walked with them, they remembered the possibilities. Hope opened the door to trusting their experience, to understanding, and eventually to recognition and commitment. We too must unpack possibilities remembered in the stories told and retold of how God's anointed must pass to glory through death and how the resurrected life is a reality. In hope, we must hold open the vision of the kingdom.

In the light of Easter, it is clear that the sacraments of initiation do not solve all of the neophytes' problems or grant them immunity from gigantic evils like injustice, hate, loneliness, and death. Rather, the promise of resurrection is found in the surprising and redeeming presence of Christ in the midst of death and denial, open graves and morning gardens, dusty roads and dark depression, along the way in walk and word, and in bonding and broken bread. It is in mystagogy that we learn to name these saving moments and trust our experiences. Without this mystagogical insight, without owning these sacramental moments, the promise of resurrection becomes a hoax. And without resurrection, we are the greatest of fools; our dying shall be without hope, and our living without mission.

Beginning with Moses and All the Prophets

It's a dead give-away. The long line of prophets that has always sustained the revelation of Truth is not finished. There seems to be no end to this truth-telling. No doubt about it, the divine encounter is a heritage of prophecy. But witnessing to the truth got the prophets of old ostracized, ridiculed, hated, and killed. The greatest prophet of all was crucified, and prophecy hasn't become any more popular today, either. It is best we brace for it.

The call to prophecy is an essential part of the message of mystagogia. Week after week we hear in Acts the brave prophetic deeds that seeded the infant church. It is no less vital for the life of the church now. However, being a "non-prophet" organization, as Jim Dunning loves to phrase it, is a tempting posture for the church today. Without persecution, with a *laissez-faire* mentality, it is easy to assume that all is well, that we live in a Christian environment. Nothing could be farther from the truth. Christianity is by its very nature a radical, counter-cultural position. Christian maturity is a call to prophecy, a tomb-opening operation in which we risk the stench for the sake of resurrection.

He interpreted every passage. Christ himself is the interpretation of every person's passage. The disciples' passage and our passage can only make sense in Christ. The disciples didn't realize it, but the Word incarnated in them, and they became new prophets in a long heritage of prophecy. In fact, they became *our* prophets. And now out of their pain, we hear our own story, our hearts begin to burn, and we recognize Christ in our midst. And so, as it was in the beginning, it is now—we prophets are another beginning.

Stay with Us

What if the disciples had never invited the Lord to stay, had not pressed him to accept their invitation? How would the story have ended then? Would they ever have recognized him? Would they have come to know him? The answers to these questions remain hidden in the mystery of God. One thing I know: willingness to invite God in might make the difference between hope and despair.

"Stay with us" is a function of prayer. That is the one thing each person must do for his or her own salvation: open the door and invite the Lord to stay. As has already been noted, we can pray *for* others but never *in place* of another. We cannot invite Christ into somebody else's life. What we can and must do is encourage the neophytes to develop a robust, hardy, "pressing" prayer life. For the neophytes, as for all of us, staying power for the Christian life is found in prayer. If all that we have done together, the story telling, the rites, even the sacraments of initiation, do not bear fruit in true prayer—transformation in the presence of the Lord—it is all for nothing. It is all undone. "Stay with us" is the essential invitation.

Their Eyes Were Opened...
in the Breaking of the Bread

These are almost magical words for us. The minute we hear them, we have that sort of "aha" sense even if we're not quite sure what we are aha-ing! In a moment of extreme honesty, we might admit that "the breaking of the bread" is a phrase mystified and romanticized into a sort of spiritual wonderland of pleasant but uncertain meaning. It makes us feel good but doesn't do much for our understanding.

Because it is Christ himself who gives it meaning, the Eucharist shall never be impotent. But our understanding of its mystery can certainly have its highs and lows, and opening of our eyes can thus be in jeopardy. It is good for us to remember with the disciples that evening meal at Emmaus. It was simple; there was nothing magic about it. Here are the elements of the happening: they invited him to stay, they sat down to eat, he pronounced the blessing, broke the bread, and began to distribute it to those around the table. In that common ritual, they recognized Jesus, though he was no longer there. They recognized him because eating with and identifying with the outcast and downtrodden is *what he always did*. Their recognition arose out of their experience of him. Broken bread symbolizes, sacramentalizes, Christ because in a real way it is a part of who he is.

My mother spent twenty-seven years in a wheelchair after a crippling stroke. But at age eighty-three she was still very much attuned to life. She loved to be around kids, politics, and football games. My husband, Don, loved to be around her. To that end, he would bet on football games with her just for the fun of watching her win, which she did with astonishing regularity. They used to place their quarter bets on the base of a lamp that sat on a table between them. The pile of quarters on her side of the lamp grew noticeably larger than his. When my mother died, Don carefully carried the lamp to our house, quarters and all. That lamp with quarters piled higher on one side was a sacrament of my mother for him. The mystery is not that my mother was made present in that lamp. Such things are common in human experience. The mystery is my mother and in how an eighty-three-year-old in a wheelchair touched lives and brought life to others.

Similarly, it is no mystery that Christ was made present for the disciples in the breaking of the bread. Such was their experience of him. The mystery is Christ, how he transformed their lives, how he transforms our lives, bringing life out of death. The revelation of that mystery, the deep remembering, the knowing again ought to move us to wonder, to celebration, and to mission. Experience touched and made present transforms living.

For us no less than the neophytes the question is this: Is the breaking of the bread a sacrament rooted in our *real experience* of Christ, or is it simply a mystical formula recognizant of nothing but religious feelings? Sacraments cannot make present to us a Christ we have not known. Recognition requires prior cognition. The mystery is not the question of real presence but the question of the real Christ. They recognized *him* in the breaking.

Heartburn

For Cleopas and his companion, the breaking open of the Scriptures raised hope and renewed fidelity. The breaking of the bread brought union. Their mystagogical experience resulted in burning hearts and clarity of mission. The mystagogical experience of many neophytes is more likely to produce confusion and heartburn. We break open the doors to ministry instead of to Scripture, and the deep remembering of presence is eradicated in the race to sign up.

The culprit in mystagogia is not ministry. The culprit is heart failure: the failure to inflame hearts with fiery Word and passionate love. We still cling to the quiet conviction that initiation is really graduation and that the job is done with pouring the water, dabbing the oil, and receiving the bread. If you experience the feeling of having to push your way through mystagogia, of having to "manufacture" reasons to be there, it is because you can't fool your innards. Call it what you like, but if your guts tell you it's graduation, it is all over. If you're done, you're done. There is nothing left to do but get 'em a job and roll up your sleeves for the next "class." That's how mystagogia dies and ministry turns into job placement. Opened eyes and inflamed hearts create the ambiance for action, not vice versa. The disciples *ran* back to proclaim the good news once they experienced the Lord. They didn't have to be prodded into anything. Knowing what to do is not a problematic decision. It is a natural response to what we have come to know and believe. Taking time to experience what we know and believe is the key to burning hearts and willing witness.

They Returned to Jerusalem

What if, when the two disciples ran back to Jerusalem, the apostles ignored them? What if the apostles didn't greet them with, "The Lord is indeed raised!"? What if the disciples were unable to share their remarkable experience? Would their faith have operated on "automatic"? I think not. Faith is deeply involved in relationship. The first instinct of these disciples was to run back to Jerusalem, to share their renewed faith, and to bolster the faith of their own community. Christian faith outside of communal affirmation has doubtful validity. The authenticity of our faith is always found in collegiality and common witness. The promise of Christ's presence is given to the gathering, the assembly of his people. An essential mystagogical enterprise is bonding with the community through shared witness. If the community is out of touch with the neophytes, mystagogia is at risk. At this time more than any other time in the whole initiation process, the community is on as the primary minister.

Somehow, we miss the naturalness of all this. We feel embarrassed to gleefully exclaim to the neophytes, "The Lord is raised indeed! Suzie has experienced resurrection!" By the same token, the new disciples are reticent to share their marvelous encounter and how they have come to know him in the breaking of the bread. Yet in other circumstances, it is instinctive to share good news. We should expect them to return to us bursting with excitement. And like the apostles, we should be waiting with good news of our own. How unnatural it is to be blasé and uninterested. How ridiculous it is to assume that we don't need their fresh vitality to sustain our own faith life! In communities where sharing and bonding does not occur and is not sought, one wonders whether the faith experience of that community and of those neophytes is simply unauthentic or whether, like everything else symbolic in our life, their faith has been smeared and bleared with toil and trade until one can no longer touch its bare beauty.

The essence of Easter is the witnessing to the resurrection experience. Be assured that if the neophytes have experienced resurrection at all, they must first return to Jerusalem, to their root community. Will they find their apostolic church waiting, faithful, and filled with the presence of the Lord? The resolution of the Emmaus encounter is not the breaking of the bread, but a witnessing community. Sacrament is for the sake of transformation; transformation erupts in mission.

For Discussion

- Read the Gospel of Luke account of the Emmaus story (Lk 24:13-35). When have you been one of the two disciples on the road? What are the questions that you ask? What puzzles you about the sacraments? about the mission of Jesus Christ? What are your hopes that have been dashed by events beyond your control? To whom do you go for comfort? for support? How do you recognize Christ?

- What does it mean to say: "Sacrament is for the sake of transformation; transformation erupts in mission"?

The Rite Application

This is it; we have come full circle. We began with the community, who by the witness of its life called inquirers into its midst. And now the integrating newcomers, as a bit of yeast in a doughy mass, gives rise to renewed life and witness within the community, which again, as leaven for the world, calls others into union and resurrection.

The rite is specific about how this intercommunion shall occur (RCIA 244):

1. This final period is a time for the community and the neophytes to learn from each other a deeper understanding of the paschal mystery.

2. This is accomplished by mutual meditation on the Gospel, sharing eucharist and doing works of charity.

3. The community, especially the godparents and pastors should support and nurture the neophytes with thoughtful and friendly assistance.

Moreover, the rite describes the inner journey of the neophytes as an induction into deeper understanding of the mysteries of the Gospel, particularly through their experience of sacrament. They are people truly renewed by the sweet taste of God in Word and Eucharist and by the indwelling of the Spirit. Out of this experience—which belongs to all Christians—arise new perceptions, a new way of understanding the church and the world, and a renewed and enlightened faith (RCIA 245). Through increased interaction, the community itself participates in this journey of newness. By sharing in a common story, in a common meal, and in common service, the entire church experiences resurrection, transformation, and Christian maturation.

Growing Together

Growth assumes two things: a normal, healthy life and the nurturing of it. Growing together further assumes that these conditions exist for both the neophytes and the community and that they have the opportunity to interact with each other. Isolation is the enemy of human growth and maturity. We know that a baby isolated from human contact can suffer retardation or even death as a result. Somehow we assume that spiritual growth is not a human process, as if faith somehow disembodies us. We privatize our spiritual journey and thereby invite the possibility of spiritual retardation and maybe even death. If we are to grow at all, we must grow together. Life in and of itself is a communal affair. It is no wonder mystagogy is difficult for us. It challenges the lie of individualism.

The health of the assembly can be measured by its corporality (i.e., whether its members function cooperatively for the life of the whole). An aggregation of bodies bent on praying does not constitute community. Neither does an assemblage of people with compatible tastes, who enjoy one another's company, constitute community. Healthy corporality envisions more than common interests, more than mere cooperation, satiation, and preservation. It seeks regeneration.

Mutual Meditation on the Gospel and Shared Eucharist

According to the rite, the locus for the mystagogical experience is the Masses for the neophytes, that is, the Sunday Masses of the Easter season (RCIA 247). The Easter lectionary (particularly that of cycle A) within the eucharistic liturgy is a fundamental component of this final period in the catechumenate. But because they are no longer dismissed after the homily, the neophytes often are given no opportunity to break open the Word. The power of the Easter lectionary is lost. What an enormous loss it is!

The Scripture of the Easter season unfolds in rich parable and marvelous deeds what it means to be a eucharistic people. It proclaims a life of mutual support and common meals, of faith more splendid than fire-tried gold, of peace and power, of Word shared and fruitful, of deliverance and brave prophecy. The Book speaks of familiar voices and sheepfolds shepherded to safety. It retells the Emmaus story and assures us that the Lord will indeed reveal himself in the breaking of the bread. It reminds us that we are living stones, an edifice of spirit built upon the unshakable cornerstone of Christ for the upbuilding of the kingdom of light. And we are assured that we have not become children of God only to be orphaned but that God's Spirit will hold us in love and in life for the sake of the regeneration of the world. The Word leads us to the eucharistic mandate: we do all this in deep memory of him.

Catechumenate teams expend a great deal of energy devising ways to present and interpret ministry to the neophytes, overlooking the splendid presentation already provided in the Easter lectionary. Without the Word, the eucharistic life is without foundation and direction. "The preaching of the word is necessary for the sacramental ministry. For sacraments are sacraments of faith and faith has its origin and sustenance in the word" (*Lectionary for Mass: Introduction* 10). How else shall we know him in the breaking of the bread?

The content, if you will, of this part of the initiation process is not simply unpacking the experience of the initiatory sacraments at the Easter Vigil. Rather, it is the exploration of the implications of initiation for the rest of our living, the unpacking through the filter of the Word of the eucharistic commitment and the eucharistic mission: "Do this" and "Go, you are sent."

New Perceptions

The rite notes that out of the sacramental experience, the neophytes "derive a new perception of the faith, the church and the world" (RCIA 245). When Alice leaned through the looking glass, she found everything she presumed about life to be reversed. Right was left, left was right, issues and values were topsy-turvy; she learned to expect the unexpected. *Through the Looking-Glass* may be a whimsical tale, but it can suggest much to us about the radical new vision of Christianity. The Gospel does not reflect American middle-class values; our ways are upended. Like Alice's adventure, initiation into Christ is an adventure into mayhem: all our facile assumptions are rendered "N.A.," "not applicable." Righteousness is relinquished in favor of common life, poverty is a treasure, success is foolishness, life springs from death, and the personal struggle for salvation gives way to commitment to kingdom living. It is mayhem that issues in mystery, the mystery of a Creator God who did not cling to being God, who took up the life of creaturehood and transformed it into a new creation by never letting go of it.

New perception is a result of passage. It always requires repositioning of some sort. Hopefully, passage has been going on throughout the entire initiatory process in a gradual, step-by-step approach as enjoined by the rite. "Leaning into life" describes well the new posture of a life of faith. Leaning is a scary sort of repositioning. It risks being off balance, being out of control; it takes trust and it implies a certain eagerness to press on. Leaning is an eschatological position; its resolution is yet to come; it is future oriented. Its perspective is hopeful. Hopefully the result is people of new vision, who see in a way they have not seen before.

The First Anniversary and Its Year

The rite calls for a full year of thoughtful and friendly help for the "newly planted." Planning this year of mystagogy ought to be a mutual vision of both team and neophytes. Now is the time the neophytes begin in earnest to take over the responsibility for their Christian maturation. Their hopes and their needs ought to be the stuff of this year's agenda. Pentecost is a good time to invoke the Spirit's counsel in discerning the direction this ground-breaking year will take. The team should listen deeply. The surface suggestions, "Wouldn't it be nice...?" or "I'd like to...," do not always represent the real needs, the deeper hungers. Such hungers are surfaced in mutual prayer and covenanted relationships. We need to pray *with* them for enlightenment.

The rite also assumes the celebration of the anniversary of their baptism. We celebrate birthdays for the sake of life. They are literally life anniversaries. It would seem barbarian and ungrateful not to mark the completion of each year of life. More than that, it is simply the natural thing to do; it arises spontaneously out of the joy of being alive. Yet we have to be told, even prodded and pushed, to celebrating the gift of life that overcomes death itself. Perhaps we honestly do not accept as fact the reality of Christ alive in us. It is more metaphor than truth for us, even though we want to believe it and do accept it in theory. But we own it in our innards only vaguely and at peak moments. Perhaps through the celebration of the Christ-life in others, we shall begin to accept it more fully in our own case. It's that business of growing together. One thing I know. Celebrating life is an important means of finding and building hope. It ought not to be neglected.

We do not celebrate life with those whom we have not first shared life. Celebration is a kind of covenant. It arises out of moments of mutuality and holds the promise of future fidelity. We celebrate the neophytes' first anniversary because we have seen them through it, nurtured their growth and maturity, and because we are bound at a shared table to uphold their life. Those of us who are faithful to our ministry will make every effort to support the neophytes in this celebration of their anniversary. But the mystagogues, those who understand the sacramental underpinnings of the Christian mission, wouldn't miss it for the world.

The Wider Church

Lest our understanding of a eucharistic community become too parochial, too self-invested, the last instruction of the rite regarding the neophytes is an injunction to the bishop. He is their pastor; they belong to a wider community. Hence the bishop is enjoined to make every effort to meet the neophytes and celebrate Eucharist with them, especially if he was unable to preside at the sacraments of initiation himself (RCIA 251). No doubt this may require a major effort on the part of the bishops of some dioceses. But if it can happen for Election, it can happen for the sake of incorporation into the larger church. The local catechumenate teams should, with one mind and heart throughout the diocese, press for the fulfillment of this right and privilege of the neophytes. The opportunity to be with and to bond with the presbyter of the diocesan community can be a door-opening symbol, a way to participate in the sacramental nature of the church itself. Celebrating Eucharist with the bishop suggests a broader, more complete sense of what it means to be eucharistic people. Significantly, the rite specifically instructs that at this eucharistic celebration the complete, full sign of Eucharist shall be used; all shall be offered both bread and cup at the communion table.

For Discussion

- Read RCIA 244-251. What are the elements found in these paragraphs? How are you incorporating these elements with the neophytes?

- How are you supporting the neophytes as they live this new life as a member of the church? as a disciple of Jesus Christ? What are the challenges that each is facing?

- In what ways does the parish welcome them into full membership and discipleship? How are they incorporated in the mission of Jesus Christ to "proclaim freedom to the captive, sight for blind, release for the oppressed"?

- How does what you do with and for the neophytes say that their status is changed, that "they are now one of us"?

The Rite Mentality

During the great fifty days of Easter, for the full mystagogical year, and for the entire life of a Catholic Christian, the central rite is eucharistic liturgy. At the table of Word and bread, the people of God remember and become what they are. The ultimate significance of the eucharistic rite has been examined and expounded in countless volumes, and still we are never quite sure of even its primal impact as we apply this mystery to our own flesh and blood in daily living. When, however, in moments of deep consciousness, we surrender to the mystery these symbols hold, we find ourselves in "the storm center of the universe," caught up in the dying and rising Christ who relinquished life, even life as God, for the sake of surrender to the mind and will of the Creator God. It is in such bush-burning moments of revelation that we stand bare-footed before the real mystery of Christian living.

Ultimately, the whole of Christian life is mystagogical: seeking and surrendering to the mysteries trying to break through to us in the symbolizing activity of our sacraments. Perhaps we have now identified the center of our real fears about mystagogia. It recalls the gutsy commitment of our Christianity. That storm center, the eye of calm, is only reached through the frightening upheaval of self-emptying, the surrender of our grasping need for ego-centric survival. If, in memory of him, we do as Christ has done, we must be ground as wheat to be food for others. We must die. This is the ultimate ritual, the dance of our salvation.

> Dance, dance, wherever you may be.
> I am the Lord of the dance, said he
> ("Lord of the Dance," Old Shaker Tune).

The Great Rite of Liturgical Time

Time is a great human ritual. Morning to night, week to week, season to season, the spiral of time marks the journey of birth to death and birth again renewed. It is the sacrament of human regeneration. Time marks the eventual unfolding of life and threads it together with memory, without which time becomes schizophrenic, devoid of rootedness, meaning, and purpose. But in the celebration of time remembered, we discover the thrust by which each moment flows into the next and creates a new reality.

Ritual is memory in action. It visibly calls into presence once again a prior experience, affirming it and raising it to a new consciousness here and now. In this way, ritual brings into being that which it symbolizes, creating a new, more intense experience out of the old. It perpetuates that essential thrust by which we create again and more intensely who we are. Ritual which bears upon the sacred is what we call sacrament.

The Hebrews believed all the world to be a revelation of God and saw all of life as sacred ritual. The initiation process is built on this sacramental understanding of life. The whole process is a sacred rite; every moment is a theophany, a revelation of God: the telling and re-telling of the story, the ritualizing of each and every step along the way, the culmination in the great night of regeneration in which the elect, in deep memory of who they have become, become more intensely who they are, Christ. Like life itself, initiation is a step-by-step unfolding of eventual becoming which does not happen all at once. Without this sacramental sense of time, initiation becomes a schizophrenic succession of events, without purpose or meaning.

Mystagogia, stretching as it does into the whole of life, depends more crucially than any other period in the initiation process on a sacramental sense of time. Becoming a mature Christian does not all happen with the pouring of the water or the fragrant flow of chrism or a single shared meal. Becoming fully Christian happens in repeated and deep remembering of who we have become and carrying that becoming with intensity into each future moment. The Eucharist is the central rite of mystagogia, but the pattern or paradigm of mystagogia is sacramental time—the liturgical seasons of the church in which we mark the sacred journey of birth to death and birth renewed. The liturgical year is the sacrament of Christian living regenerated again and again. It is a gift given in the mystagogical year. It is a gift for life.

For Discussion

- Two key statements to return to time and again are:

  Ritual is memory in action. It visibly calls into presence once again a prior experience, affirming it and raising it to a new consciousness here and now (page 172).

  The initiation process is built on this sacramental understanding of life. The whole process is a sacred rite; every moment is a theophany, a revelation of God: the telling and re-telling of the story, the ritualizing of each and every step along the way, the culmination...in which

the elect...become more intensely who they are, Christ
(page 172-3).

- How does each of you on the team continue to grow
  in your own understanding of what it means to "be
  Christ"? How does your parish understand its role to
  "be Christ"?

- Return to the ritual text again and again. Read it,
  pray it, discuss it. You will never reach the end
  because each time you read it, you are a different
  person and the inquirers are new. Pray that your team
  continues to be involved in the conversion dynamic.
  Be faithful to Christ rather than successful in
  developing a program.

Works Cited

Caroluzza, Thomas. Address delivered at the Forum Seminar for RCIA
  Leadership Development at Loyola University, Chicago, July 1988.

Constitution on the Sacred Liturgy. Washington, DC: International
  Committee on English in the Liturgy, 1982.

Cooney, Rory. "You in Our Day." *Mystery.* Phoenix: North American
  Liturgy Resources, 1987.

Dick, Michael Brennan. "Conversion in the Bible." *Conversion and the
  Catechumenate.* Edited by Robert Duggan. New York: Paulist Press, 1984.

Dunning, James. "What Happens after 'Christ Among Us'?" *Forum* 1, no.
  4. (1984).

Empereur, James. *Exploring the Sacred.* Washington, DC: The Pastoral Press,
  1987.

Environment & Art in Catholic Worship. Washington, DC: United States
  Catholic Conference, 1978.

Fowler, James W. *Stages of Faith.* San Francisco: Harper & Row Publishers
  Inc., 1981.

Fragomeni, Richard. "Lent, Holy Week and Easter Season." Address given
  at the First Convocation of the North American Forum on the
  Catechumenate, Washington, DC, 1987.

General Norms for the Liturgical Year. Washington, DC: International
  Committee on English in the Liturgy, 1982.

The Good News According to Matthew. Translated by Edward Schwizer and David Greene. Atlanta: John Knox Press, 1975.

Huck, Gabe. *The Three Days*. Chicago: Liturgy Training Publications, 1981.

Kavanagh, Aidan. "Christian Initiation: Tactics and Strategy," *Made, Not Born*.

——. "Christian Initiation of Adults: The Rites." *Made, Not Born*.

——. *The Shape of Baptism*. New York: Pueblo, 1978.

Keating, Thomas. *Open Mind, Open Heart*. Warwick, New York: Amity House Inc., 1986.

Keifer, Ralph A. "Christian Initiation: The State of the Question." *Made, Not Born*.

Kemp, Ray. "The Mystagogical Experience." *Christian Initiation Resource Reader*. Vol. 4. New York: Wm. H. Sadlier Press, 1984.

Lectionary for Mass: Introduction. Washington, DC: International Committee on English in the Liturgy, 1969.

Lumen Gentium (Dogmatic Constitution on the Church). In *Vatican Council II: The Conciliar and Post Conciliar Documents*. Edited by Austin Flannery, OP. Northport, NY: Costello Publishing Co., 1975.

Made, Not Born: New Perspectives on Christian Initiation and the Catechumenate. Notre Dame: University Press, 1959.

McBrien, Richard P. *Catholicism*. Study Edition. San Francisco: Harper & Row Publishers Inc., 1981.

Music in Catholic Worship. Washington, DC: United States Catholic Conference, 1983.

National Statutes for the Catechumenate. Washington, DC: National Conference of Catholic Bishops, 1986.

O'Dea, Barbara. *Of Fast & Festival*. Ramsey, New Jersey: Paulist Press, 1982.

Rite of Christian Initiation of Adults. Washington, DC: United States Catholic Conference, 1985.

Shea, John. *The God Who Fell from Heaven*. Allen, Texas: Argus Communications, 1979.

Stokes, Kenneth, ed. *Faith Development in the Adult Life Cycle*. New York: W. H. Sadlier, 1983.

Taft, Robert. *The Liturgy of the Hours in East and West*. Collegeville, Minnesota: The Liturgical Press, 1986.

Theological Dictionary of the New Testament. 10 vols. Edited by Gerhard Kittel. Translated by Geoffrey W. Bromiley. Grand Rapids, Michigan: Wm. B. Eerdmans Publishing Co., 1974.

Untener, Bishop Kenneth. "What Kind of Church Does the Rite Want?" Paper delivered at the Omni-Shoreham Hotel, Washington, DC, September 1987.

Wallis, Jim. *The Call to Conversion.* San Francisco: Harper & Row Publishers Inc., 1981.

Westley, Dick. *Morality and Its Beyond.* Mystic, Connecticut: Twenty-Third Publications, 1984.

STORIES FOR CATECHESIS

PARABLES OF CONVERSION
Homilies and Stories Based on the Lectionary

Lou Ruoff
Paper, 128 pages, 5½" x 8½", 0-89390-403-1

"Everyone, it seems, has a favorite Father Lou homily. The one about the Lone Ranger, complete with theme song. The time he brought a sheep to the altar. The one about his buddy in Philly who tattooed his girlfriend Sue's name all over his body and ended up marrying a girl named Sharon." —The Virginian-Pilot and the Ledger-Star.

Father Lou is back — this time with stories focused on the conversion experience. To make a point about conversion, look into *Parables of Conversion*. Some are narratives, others more poetic. Some are dialogue, others are reflections that occur only within one's heart of hearts. Some are fantasy, others help you experience what it is like to live in the gutter with the muck of humanity. But each tale relates a set of experiences that lead, through grace, to a moment of conversion. And each parable poses a spiritual question while remaining open-ended — the better to encourage discussion and reflection.

STORIES TO INVITE FAITH-SHARING
Experiencing the Lord Through the Seasons

Mary McEntee McGill
Paper, 128 pages, 5½" x 8 ½", 0-89390-230-6

Sharing our stories makes our faith journey easier. These twenty stories are based on real life experiences which help us recognize God's presence in everyday life. Reflections and questions for group sharing can lead to personal awareness and prayer. Great for faith-sharing groups, workshops, and retreats.

Call Toll-Free 1-888-273-7782 for current prices.
See last page for ordering information.

LECTIONARY-BASED CATECHESIS

Lead your catechumens to faith with *Celebrating The Lectionary*!

The sacramentary and the lectionary are the preferred texts for the catechumenate. It doesn't matter if you're working with children or adults. *Celebrating The Lectionary*'s Adult packet has been a mainstay for years in many parish catechumenate groups. The Children's Catechumenate packet solves a huge problem for catechists trying to work with children of mixed ages.

ADULT PACKET
Ages 18 and up

Edited by Cathy Qualls
Looseleaf, 424 pages, 8½" x 11"
Materials published annually for every Sunday of the year

Organize a weekly one-hour session for adults based on the Sunday lectionary. This catechetical resource has everything you need: seasonal and Sunday background sessions, session plans, photocopiable handouts and a handy booklet full of extra resources. Use these materials for catechumenate sessions, for lector preparation or for parent sessions conducted in concert with a children's program.

CHILDREN'S CATECHUMENATE PACKET
Ages 7–11

Edited by Cathy Qualls
Looseleaf, 452 pages, 8½" x 11"
Materials published annually for every Sunday of the year

Celebrating The Lectionary's Children's Catechumenate packet is loaded with resources that will help you catechize around the lectionary. For each Sunday you'll get Sunday Background Sheets commenting on the readings, session plans with plenty of options for older and younger children and a Parent and Child Sharing Sheet. Includes optional summer session plans and photocopiable masters.

Call Toll-Free 1-888-273-7782 for current prices.
See last page for ordering information.

Discover your parish's most powerful catechetical tool ...

If you only had a resource that could effectively form the faith of everyone in your community — babies, teenagers, adults, seniors.

Liturgical Catechesis shows you how to use a tool you already have — the liturgy.

Six times a year this information-packed magazine will give you background, ideas, tips and the expertise you need to make catechesis come alive for everyone in your community.

Since the church has mandated that all catechesis should be "modeled on the baptismal catechumenate," you can't afford to be without this valuable aid to your ministry.

Don't miss the next issue. Visit www.liturgicalcatechesis.com and request your no-risk trial subscription to *Liturgical Catechesis* magazine. We guarantee you'll find this magazine indispensable.